OXF
IND
INTRODUCTIONS

INDIAN NATIONAL SECURITY

The Oxford India Short
Introductions are concise,
stimulating, and accessible guides
to different aspects of India.
Combining authoritative analysis,
new ideas, and diverse perspectives,
they discuss subjects which are
topical yet enduring, as also
emerging areas of study and debate.

OTHER TITLES IN THE SERIES

For more information, visit our website:
https://india.oup.com/content/series/o/
oxford-india-short-introductions/

OXFORD
INDIA SHORT
INTRODUCTIONS

INDIAN
NATIONAL
SECURITY

CHRIS OGDEN

OXFORD
UNIVERSITY PRESS

Oxford University Press is a department of the University of Oxford.
It furthers the University's objective of excellence in research, scholarship,
and education by publishing worldwide. Oxford is a registered trademark of
Oxford University Press in the UK and in certain other countries.

Published in India by
Oxford University Press
2/11 Ground Floor, Ansari Road, Daryaganj, New Delhi 110 002, India

ISBN-13: 978-0-19-946647-4
ISBN-10: 0-19-946647-5

Typeset in 11/14.3 Bembo Std
by Excellent Laser Typesetters, Pitampura, Delhi 110 034
Printed in India by Replika Press Pvt. Ltd

for Orfeas

Contents

Figures

Preface

India is a country of increasing domestic complexity and mounting international importance. As she rises to prominence, this Oxford India Short Introduction provides an invaluable introduction to both the internal and external aspects of her national security. In an increasingly interdependent and globalizing world, appreciating the interests and principles structuring India's national security has never been so important, in particular how they relate to *international* security issues.

Moving away from a solely traditional focus upon borders, military power, internal stability, and protecting against invasion, national security now involves non-traditional tenets such as trade, energy, and environmental security. Importantly, it has also become more comprehensive, with a focus on critical infrastructure, food and water access, international diplomacy, disaster and humanitarian relief, as well as recognizing the threat posed by non-state actors—especially from terrorism, piracy, and even transnational corporations. Embracing such a multifaceted analysis of national security not only serves to highlight the diverse challenges facing India, but also stresses the impact that they will have on her current global rise. In these ways, this book:

- *enriches* our understanding of national security in India, vitally enhancing our knowledge base regarding the range of internal and external threats faced by her leaders and people;
- *generates* a fuller appreciation of what is meant by national security in the twenty-first century, including an investigation into its current non-traditional and non-state actor aspects; and
- *examines* India's crucial positioning at the fulcrum of many contemporary global security threats, and details the impact such threats will have on her national policy and behaviour.

Introduction

Thinking about National Security

In recent years, national security has emerged as
one of the most pervasive terms within politics and
international affairs, both inside and outside of India.
Referring to the maintenance of a country's survival
and well-being against a range of seemingly existential threats, the scale of national security has grown
in scope and stature to encompass virtually all aspects
of a country's security concerns. At the core of these
understandings is a country's ability—and the nation it
embodies—to protect itself from others so as to ensure
complete self-reliance and self-sufficiency.

Freedom from threat, in whatever form that threat
may take—both actual and imagined—is at the root of
these conceptions. So, too, is the capacity of leaders to
preserve their country's physical nature and integrity,
protect its form of governance and core institutions,

and uphold its guiding national values and principles, so as to collectively preserve the way of life of its citizens. These elements represent the uniqueness of a country, the essence of which is innately threatened by other countries, actors, behaviours, interests, perspectives, and even ideas that differ from them. Within all these parameters, the preservation and defence of territory most typically trumps all other issues.

The origin of such threats to a country can be both external and internal—from the enemy without and the enemy within—and these threats by definition seek to disrupt, unsettle, and ultimately destabilize the country. Such threats (and the actors embodying or invoking them) aim to dilute or threaten national cohesion to the detriment of its leaders, peoples, borders, and values. It is the role of a country's leaders to resist such coercion, to develop the necessary security apparatuses central to such resistance, and to actively maintain their national independence by whatever means they can. In these ways, national security is both a negative as well as a positive concept; in that it simultaneously aims to protect against any destabilizing threats in order to preserve the way of life of a country.

Ensuring national security pivots around the protection of national interests—that is, the key goals, objectives, and policy preferences that a country has concerning its desired international and national self-image. These determinants then serve to guide a country's behaviour. These are also central to state sovereignty and state legitimacy, in that the fulfilment of these interests is the ongoing test of the effectiveness or not of their ruling elites. Within the modern international system, the protection of society from threats forms a core responsibility of governments via powerful sovereign leaders who rule on behalf of their populations so as to fulfil this promise.

This responsibility is the motivation for the application of a country's power in the global sphere, whereby international engagement can heighten the maintenance of national security. It also indicates how any country is fundamentally a self-centred entity, whereby its interests and their fulfilment or protection will, at the most basic level of survival, necessarily take precedence over others. Within this perspective, the study and analysis of national security is innately specific to the country under examination, and reflective not only of its core national interests but also its geopolitical location vis-à-vis others, and the range of potential enemies it faces at any given time.

Facets

Initially, national security emerged in relation to a range of traditional concerns, primarily the military means with which to protect a country's borders—both land and sea—along with any vital interests relating to economics and access to resources. Within these domains, the safeguarding of sovereignty, territory, and the population took precedence. Much of this preservation is related to maintaining a country's physical integrity and the territorial extent that embodies it, along with any offshore or colonial landmasses that it may also possess or occupy.

As part of these dynamics, war, as both an offensive and defensive means, typified national security. This understanding persisted throughout the colonial and imperial eras of world history, up until the Second World War and the consequent Cold War. Carrying out or resisting conquest was its central component, and it rested upon the ability of a country to amass and deploy physical might—in the form of armies, navies, and air forces (along with the commensurate increase in their destructive power and capacity). Such means are not only protective and preventative (say, against direct invasion by other countries), but are also tools to allow the purposeful enforcement of a particular worldview or set of national interests upon others.

In the last few decades, these facets have expanded and evolved to include more non-traditional considerations, such as energy security (the protection of access to oil and gas supplies, and other expendable

and renewable raw materials) and environmental security (to combat climate change and its consequences),
along with ensuring political and social freedom of
individuals even from a country's government (commonly referred to as human security). Access to natural
resources (water, land, and minerals) beyond a country's
immediate borders thus also forms part of the national
security remit, and can unleash internal instabilities and
conflict between countries.

To these global interests and transnational issues can
be added the broad spectrum of economic security.
This goes beyond merely ensuring energy supplies
and includes the creation and protection of national
industries and jobs, which again involves either cooperation with or safeguard from a range of external
forces. Moreover, these interests become critical to
society, whereby employment helps accumulate overall
national wealth, provides military and non-military
manpower, and maintains societal stability by the creation of employment and prosperity.

Such concerns furthermore relate to political
security that seeks to preserve social order and the
underlying values, principles, and understandings that
characterize the society of a country. These are often
crafted through the guiding visions and worldviews
of their most significant historical leaders and, most
commonly, at times of a country's initial formation

and independence. Values are also the means by which countries interact with each other through a process of simultaneously projecting/protecting their national values and principles with/against others. These values, as we will see, also play a crucial role in determining a country's national interests and providing a subjective set of preferences formed by domestic context and external conditions.

Actors

The variety and number of actors involved in the realization of national security has also increased in line with the range of potential inputs and influences. Though primarily relating to countries (including their various labels as states and nations) and their ruling elites, governments, and populations, more non-conventional foes fall within the national security sphere. These include myriad non-state actors in the guise of terrorists, separatists, insurgents, criminal organizations, political and religious activists, tribes, minorities, drug cartels, gangs, dissidents, computer hackers, and any wider groupings and associations that they may collectively form.

The increasing influence and relevance of multinational corporations can be added to this potent mix, some of which are richer than numerous countries, along with non-governmental organizations. These actors gain significance through their cross-border, transnational, and pan-global reach, and their concurrent competition for economic markets and resources. For all of these actors, the presence of 24-hour, year-round global electronic and print media has the potential to accelerate and compound the various threats that they embody. This assertion specially applies to nationalist sentiments that promote ideal images of how a country ought to be.

National security threats also include more abstract realizations, say, in the form of natural disaster or global warming, which depend upon no clear actor. These frequently transnational threats link together domestic, regional, and international spheres, as do other interests/threats such as financial security or cyber security. As such, national security concerns increasingly correspond with wider (and shared) global security issues. They also underscore the importance of information and the negative repercussions that losing it can have on political, economic, and military security, as well as how these threats are interlinked in both importance and potential impact.

Critically, what all of these actors share, through the threats and fears that they embody, is that of being potential *existential* dangers that menace the myriad aspects making up a country's identity. Containing both tangible and intangible aspects—in that some threats are real and others simply imagined—our understanding of national security rests upon highlighting those elements that are more material and those which are more perceptual, or a combination of the two. What constitutes national security, and the threats towards it, thus reflects the wider world in which we live but depends upon the meanings given to it, is open to interpretation, and evolves over time.

It is for these reasons, as Arnold Wolfers pertinently notes, that national security remains as 'an ambiguous symbol meaning different things to different people. National security objectively means the absence of threats to acquired values, and subjectively the absence of fear that such values will be attacked' (Wolfers 1952).

Tools

A specific country's diverse, subjective, and pluralistic preferences concerning how best to achieve national security is realized through various tools to combat any purported threats. Just as a country's national security outlook is determined by the overriding perceptions of policymakers at any given time, such tools are value-laden. This weighing then influences the importance that they are given, how they are understood, and the way in which they are ultimately deployed. As threats and actors evolve, the composite mélange of these tools also gestates and adapts in nature.

The most immediate tools for any country to develop are security forces such as armies, navies, air forces, police services, and civil defence groupings. These can be deployed to combat external and internal threats, as well as to protect borders, quell internal instability, and to project control beyond a country's physical confines. Modernizing such assets, along with periodically upgrading critical infrastructure (primarily, roads, railways, bridges, communication networks, and power supplies) also forms part of this process. Their scale ultimately depends on a country's territorial extent, the length of her land and sea borders, and the number and size of her neighbours. Having access to the means to adequately pay for such tools is of further paramount significance.

Countries also develop internal and external intelligence services to use espionage to detect, deter, and defeat threats, and to protect state secrets (via classified information). Counter-intelligence activities (collecting information to deter espionage by other countries and actors) complement such actions, as do the state surveillance of domestic (and foreign) populations and their communications. Effective use of media bodies can also be used to disseminate key messages to the population. Economic power, vital to funding and maintaining all of these abilities, can also facilitate (or compel) cooperation with other actors through mutually beneficial trade or aid relations. At the highest level, countries use diplomacy to highlight common security issues and create alliances, and use such connections to isolate shared threats against their mutual interests.

Elements of control are, therefore, central to all of these national security tools and techniques, both as a means to combat threats and as a means to preserve a country's internal attributes. In these ways, the ability to regulate domestic and foreign conditions is of paramount importance so as to ensure continued autonomy, self-determination, and, in many cases, prosperity. Without these fundamentals, the very identity of a country will be threatened, potentially weakened, and ultimately dissolved—a process that removes its distinctiveness in the international sphere. Without a source of threat, the raison d'être for any government/ grouping to rule that country as the guarantor of its national survival can appear under question, undercutting its legitimacy.

Approach

As any country's national security proclivities depend on her specific values, geopolitical location, historical experiences, and her decision-makers' preferences, this book utilizes an approach from international relations theory called constructivism. Constructivism is premised upon the importance of culture and identity for explaining the behaviour of countries. Specific cultural and political beliefs and assumptions form the basis of such identities and preferences, which are then produced (or constructed) through interaction, principally between countries and their leaders.

This approach contrasts with other popular approaches within international relations, such as differing forms of realism that predominantly deem only military power to be the most important factor of consideration. Within such a perspective, all countries are regarded as having the same outlook concerning the world and of having the same aim of maximizing their power relative to others. This is primarily done through attaining more material as opposed to ideational (identity-based) resources. Such accounts ignore the relevance of internal factors such as explicit cultural or social traits, and eschew giving any significance to core influences such as history and memory.

The utilization of a constructivist methodology will allow us to discern what is particular and exclusive concerning the parameters, make-up, and fundamental interests central to the delineation of *Indian* national security. Resting upon a set of core principles concerning how we can understand the world, it places particular emphasis on the following five analytical attributes.

- *History*: To explain how the experiences of India's elites and population over time—from pre-1947 Independence struggle to the present day—have crafted a certain set of embedded values, principles, and behaviours that are particular to India's circumstances.
- *Identity*: These experiences, along with India's physical nature, political underpinnings, and social foundations, in turn, have collectively formed an identity specific to India. This identity evolves as India learns from other countries through continued interaction.
- *Culture*: Rather than seeing all countries as having the same national security interests, it is India's various (and multiple) cultural traits that give her—via her domestic, regional, and international environment—a particular exclusivity that informs her policy preferences.
- *Perception*: The threats and interests making up Indian national security are critically dependent upon how her policymakers perceive their internal and external environment. These perceptions dictate the scale of the challenges she faces and how to resolve them.

- *Interaction*: The contours of Indian national security are not only conditioned by how New Delhi sees the world but also how these viewpoints interact, coalesce, and diverge with the perspectives of others. It is this interplay that determines her immediate threat situation.

We furthermore utilize Abraham Maslow's hierarchy of needs to point out how national security must meet the fundamental biological, physiological, safety, esteem, and self-actualization needs of a country. The usage of this hierarchy is intended to be purely indicatory so as to show the wide range of these needs and also indicate the clear disconnect in India between the attainment of basic needs for the whole population and the grander elite-driven aims for the country to be a great power. As such, Indian national security can mean different things for different parts of her population.

Progressing from this basis, we analyse the vital aspects of India's contemporary national security, detail examples critical to its various dimensions, and highlight the ongoing threats that it faces. Chapter 1 outlines the origins of India's core security principles, national values, and vital interests. Chapter 2 then focuses on the internal dimension of her national security, primarily emphasizing on domestic and territorial influences, as well as the role of institutions and various security services. In turn, Chapter 3 assesses external elements including energy, resource, and trade security, and their interplay with military, diplomatic, and geopolitical factors. The Conclusion sums up these perspectives and discusses how dynamic evolution, learning, and adaptation are critical features regarding our appreciation of Indian national security.

1

Origins and Characteristics

Indian national security is underpinned by a set of core principles and interests. These are informed by the influence of India's earliest leaders, the state's physical location and attributes, and the important reference point of history (especially colonial). Taken together, they constitute the underlying themes and threats central to the delineation of Indian national security, and reflect the viewpoints of India's major political parties and their ideological biases. These principles are also situated within the narrative of India's contemporary development and modernization needs, prospective international rise, and increased ties with Asia and the world.

The context of India's gradual embrace of globalization—and the concurrent proliferation of non-traditional and international threats—forms an essential part of this analysis, as does the investigation of various non-state actors. Apart from providing an overview of the major security issues affecting India's policymakers, this discussion will then be deployed to structure the subsequent chapters of this book concerning the national interests and their associated threats/fears/desires typifying internal and external dimensions of Indian national security.

As per our theoretical leanings, our major emphasis will be on the post-Independence era of India from 1947, but with some appreciation of the role that the colonial period has had—and continues to have— upon successive generations of Indian elites. It is these understandings that are intrinsic to the formation of an Indian identity (with related principles, values, and culture) and directly indicate the topography of her national security interests and fears. Perception, that is, the interpretation of interactions, events, and experiences, vitally underpins this identity, especially in relation to New Delhi's outlook vis-à-vis South Asia and the wider global sphere.

Essences

To comprehend India's national security basis, we must appreciate the various influences and essence that are central to its formation, and the impact that they have had on it. For all countries this process is dependent upon its distinctive circumstances and surroundings. These allow for the formation of a specific approach concerning the realization and fulfilment of its national security. These attributes act as an essential resource concerning the values and symbols that leaders possess for organizing their populations and legitimizing their actions. These also form a temporal repository from which a country's identity is constructed and crafted.

As a continually gestating and synergistic entity, the values and overall identity typifying national security is absorptive of a country's past experiences with others and, via the (frequent) repetition of interaction, represents a settled set of habitual behaviour, preferences, and precedents. These learnt responses are then transmitted across generations by elites and policymakers, as well as the country's bureaucratic institutions, along with the wider (and conditioned) emotional basis of the wider population concerning their country. Although open to new influences, such engrained essence shapes the relatively constant core of national security.

Given that national security concerns the protection of a country from any opposition to its core national values, substance, and outlook, these elements constitute an internal *self* that involves interaction with diametrically opposed *others*, both external and internal. Hence, domestic and international spheres overlap with each other, and for a country with global interests such as India that is now dependent upon external linkages (such as trade markets, energy, and diplomacy), the necessity of this interlinkage is underlined in the book. It also confirms that national security must take place within both of these areas.

Characteristic of such perspectives, Kautilya—the author of *Arthashastra*, an ancient discourse on statecraft, economics, and military strategy dating to 350 BC— was one of the earliest analysts to recognize the interconnection of these different spheres for India. In particular, his 'mandala' concept focused upon the concentric circle of states surrounding India. Domination within such a mechanism was a key component concerning territorial consolidation, India's regional supremacy versus her immediate neighbours, and her having a sphere of influence stretching beyond her natural borders, particularly into the wider IOR. Such ideas continue to permeate the strategic thinking of India's national security experts to this day.

Seeing India's natural environment in such a way gives us an indication of the first enduring essences that formulate the basis of Indian national security and the central outlooks structuring it. National importance has informed these world views, especially India's past as an ancient civilization including the glories of the Mughal Empire (from mid-sixteenth to mid-

4

nineteenth centuries), which at its height encompassed all of South Asia. It was also at this time that India amassed nearly one quarter of the world's economic output, which not only gave her a global influence but concurrently heightened the importance of this status to her ruling elites. Even though separated by centuries, many future Indian leaders have harked back to this epoch as evidence of their country's undeniable greatness in the past but also as a precedent of the future they wish to come.

Thus, with a self-image of possessing a significant and enduring permanence to which others were attracted and accommodated, India's leaders conceived their country to be vitally encompassed with a role of global import. By extension this role linked their internal sphere with the wider external milieu. These two domains were bound together, making them of mutual national import concerning the maintenance and realization of her national security aims and interests. A desire to be a country of high international ranking only underscored this outlook, and shows how aspirations and ambition can be as critical to national security as threats and fear.

Even when some interactions with the outside world led to conquest (and later colonization by myriad external countries such as Britain, France, Portugal, and Denmark), such exchanges were regarded as being acts of eventual assimilation. As such, foreign influences were ultimately fused into, rather than diverging from, India's national identity. Such an outlook would form the initial basis for a national tolerance towards all groups and religions, as well as the ongoing efforts of leaders to seek the unity of their sovereign entity through diversity, so as to preserve 'India'. The key principles underpinning this idealistic world view included having an anti-majoritarian and secular (meaning universal and inclusive) body politic, based upon equality and liberalism.

Such notions persisted throughout Indian history and formed the modern entity that we see today, whose leaders still largely espouse the plurality for their people. In this ilk, India's first prime minister, Jawaharlal Nehru, pertinently noted that India is 'a world in itself, a culture and a civilization which gave shape to all things ... [and within which] foreign influence poured in, often influenced that culture and were absorbed' (Nehru 1946). Notwithstanding her highly varied ethnic and religious make-up, protecting and eventually enshrining these values into the Indian Constitution collectively personified Indian national security and her search for national autonomy.

The negative experience of colonial rule under the British Raj from 1847 further tempered these foundational urges, primarily in terms of the leaders who led the Independence struggle culminating in the creation of mid-twentieth-century modern India. Following on from two centuries of commercial exploitation by the East India Company, imperial rule serves as the core reference point for many of India's contemporary national security interests and issues. These range from her geographic borders and internal development to her self-image and status.

First among these influences was a renewed sense of India's international prominence and the key geographical location she had in South Asia on vital trade routes to West Asia and East Asia, as well as overland routes northwards into Afghanistan and Central Asia. Although subjugated by the British, this geostrategic importance served to underline that such a role and positioning was innate to India that necessitated a broader remit in terms of her international interaction, and a resultantly wider set of perceived national security interests and responsibilities.

At its core, India's experience of the British Raj led her elites to fear—at least in the earliest decades after Independence—external actors of any kind. This led to a world view beset by distrust of the intentions of other powers towards her. Imperial occupation thus became the fount of well-established anti-western attitudes and of a highly defensive approach in her national security, which aimed to prevent the repetition of events that

7

had deeply diminished her wealth and status. It also inculcated strong antagonism towards expansion and conquest as national security tools. Paradoxically, the withdrawal of the British in 1947 also buttressed a sense of India's longevity and ongoing ability to positively enthral and distil external influences within her national identity.

By their very nature, these simultaneous instincts underline the tensions that exist at the core of a country's national security, whereby the preservation of interests is inimically informed by the fears that they are set against, and which can then reinforce and confirm each other over time. Furthermore, this opposition highlights the interaction dynamic at the centre of our constructivist account, which increasingly ties positive and negative attributes so closely together that they often become contingent upon each other, in terms of mutual derivation and definition.

In other spheres, the period of colonial rule led to further legacies concerning the material nature and extent of India, principally in terms of her borders, issues that would be constant areas of contestation throughout her modern incarnation. Resting upon the uncertain demarcation of her boundaries in her northeastern and northwestern regions with Pakistan, China (the McMahon Line), Nepal, and Bhutan, and efforts to accurately restore and secure these areas became a key national security interest. This was concerned as much with territory as with physical self-image.

On a more fundamental level, and linked to India's precolonial standing and importance (reaffirmed by India's essentialness to the British Empire as being the 'Jewel of the Raj'), colonial rule had reduced India's material wealth, increased levels of poverty, and degraded her internal development. Restoring these elements was not only a key part of the Independence struggle but also formed the lodestone of nationalist voices and groupings that endeavoured to make the country great again. One of the most virulent strains of this nationalism would be the Bharatiya Janata Party (BJP) that has resolved to resurrect India's past status as a world-leading Hindu civilization. As the twentieth, and indeed twenty-first, century progressed, such actors emerged as major influences on the promulgation of India's core national security interests and resultant behaviour.

Domains

Further to the existence of these central guiding and initial essence, India's leaders were able to develop a particular and articulate world view concerning India's political make-up, its geographic scope and extent, and aspirant place in the world. An emphasis upon such particular, though not exhaustive, principles helps us to determine the more salient elements of Indian national security in terms of her core strategic goals, that is her national interests. These goals themselves rest upon particular desires (positive ways by which these aims can be fulfilled or the core principles maintained) and often concurrent/inverse fears and threats (negative outlooks concerning how the achievement of these aims might be curtailed, or how the core principles are being menaced).

The overriding aim of Nehru, as the principal originator of Indian foreign policy, was to pursue a policy of enlightened national self-interest. This was encapsulated by the concept of *purna swaraj* (achieving complete independence and self-reliance). It was intended to make India and by extension her elites—as those tasked to protect national sovereignty—the sole masters of national security, in terms of its conception, delivery, and prevailing behaviour. A sense of Indian uniqueness as a would-be great power in the world pervaded this search for self-sufficiency.

Mimicking the chief modus operandi of any country's national security interests but simultaneously characterized by the Indian context, Nehru based this conception upon a world vision typified by notions of peace, harmony, cooperation, development, and equality. Broader anti-colonial, anti-imperial, and

10

pro-democracy values further underpinned this approach, and served to accentuate how particular historical experiences and interactions directly inform actions and outcomes. Leading to the embodiment of the nation's will, the emotional responses of Indian leaders in terms of their attitudes, beliefs, values, memories, and self-conception thus influence this process.

In the foreign policy sphere, these understandings would subsequently translate into certain policy directions. These mainly involved promoting positive neutralism, supporting global non-alignment and calling for universal disarmament, which included nuclear weapons, as well as giving the Indian military a minimal role in the political process. Such approaches were intended to preserve India's strategic autonomy and rejected the bipolar enmity of the Cold War between the United States and former Soviet Union. Therefore, the subjective sphere linked to the practical sphere through the interlinking of values with behaviour, and in their totality, a national identity.

Elements of tolerance, non-aggression, non-interference, and non-intervention by India and also desired from others, further typified Nehruvian idealism. Again, these sentiments reflected lessons from adverse past interactions, mixed them with current strategic circumstances (mainly India's impoverishment/vulnerability in the 1940s) and then introduced

11

them as guiding policy preferences and tendencies. The realization/enactment of other core principles, such as non-violence (ahimsa) and economic self-reliance (swadeshi) followed a similar trajectory, and served to dually protect and *project* core values central to India's foreign policy (and hence national security).

Returning to the remit of national security, that is, the protection of interests essential to the continuation of a particular 'idea of India' as predominantly characterized by the Nehruvian values set out here, we are able to identify several key, if broad, domains running through it. These relate to defending her democratic and secular basis; ensuring India's sovereignty and territorial integrity; and enabling her modernization/development en route to becoming a great power. The concerns epitomizing these domains often intersect, producing an interdependent national security matrix, and form the basis of the internal/external scope of present-day Indian national security. For the purposes of this short introduction they are indicatory and not absolute.

Democracy and Secularism

The political system of modern India encapsulated the guiding principles of a socially inclusive country that was purposefully broad-minded towards all its creeds and religions. Rejecting any emphasis upon a single community and hence avoiding any communalist tendencies, this system was furthermore liberal, secular (that is, tolerant), not non-religious, socialist (courtesy of Nehru's Indian National Congress), and democratic. From this basis, the plurality of India's myriad regions, languages, and social rankings were amalgamated into an ostensibly socially unified mix. The negative national experience of Partition that led to the realization of modern India, and its schism from the exclusively Islamic modern Pakistan, emboldened these political foundations.

With Nehru holding office until his death in 1964 and dominating the making of domestic and foreign policy all that while, his guiding logic of a democratic and secular country would be closely adhered to by generations of Indian politicians and bureaucrats until the 1990s. British rule influenced how such a system functioned, as India inherited a first one after the post-electoral regime and a parliamentary form of cabinet government. Despite the inequities of the caste system, the Indian Constitution of January 1950 declared India to be a federal and non-monarchical sovereign democratic republic, with an independent judiciary, a single electorate, and guaranteed rights.

The Constitution also contained Articles such as 25(1) to ensure *sarva dharma shambhava* (equal treatment of all religions) that reflected not only Nehru's world view but also that of India's repeated historical exposure to conquering empires. Also cognizant of India being a Hindu-dominated society, Article 15(1)—no state discrimination on the grounds of religion—further sought to safeguard the customs, laws, and practices across the span of India's multiple minority cultural, religious, and social communities, and further enshrined the principle of unified equality.

In these ways, India's initial leaders regarded democracy and secularism as the means to provide a stable political foundation specific to the needs of their newly independent country, making them both primary national security interests. As per the dynamics of national security, these interests needed to be protected against anything that threatened them—in this case as represented by communalism and militancy that sought to privilege certain specific groups over secularism's unifying identity.

The mass violence of Partition that led to over a million deaths personified the potential divisiveness inherent to such differences. It acted as the paramount emotional reference point and national trauma that encapsulated the consequences of India's secular fabric being removed from her body politic. As such, this experience established a secular/communal dialectic within Indian national security that differentiated between an element of India's desired self-image and its associated threat/fear. In many ways, this threat was an anti-image to be avoided at all costs.

Militancy by ethnic and other groups seeking independence and accession away from the Indian state similarly represented an ideological threat to the all-inclusive vision of elites in New Delhi. Such groupings embodied major threats towards India's internal political stability, which had the potential to disrupt and weaken the country and expose it to other external or foreign threats. Confronting this fear resulted in the Indian government's highly unyielding approach towards potential separatists, whose high incidence served to engrain them into national security thinking.

Separatists in the North-East, such as the 1960s Mizo, Naga, and Gharo freedom movements, and Assam, or more contemporary insurgent groups such as Naxalites, all personify this fear. Other threats have included Punjabi Sikhs attempting to create an independent Khalistan (Land of the Pure) during the 1980s and 1990s, and Tamils in the south demanded self-rule in the 1950s and 1960s. The deployment of the Indian military against these threats acted as a vital national security tool.

Elsewhere, the contested status of Kashmir with Pakistan from 1947 until the present day has expressed similar fears. Insurgency in the region dating from

1989, and aided by Pakistan's connivance (itself representing a rival political form), further produced protracted threats to India's democratic secularism, plurality, and tolerance. Exacerbated ethnic tensions have, in turn, enhanced the prospect of communal violence and insurgency taking place in other states in India, with the insurgency spilling over, primarily in the North-East. Such unrest has also often linked up with India's criminal underworld, involving them in communal violence, frequently in Mumbai.

Many examples reveal the threat posed by communalism and militancy towards national security, and personify its persistence. These include the 31 October 1984 assassination of Prime Minister Indira Gandhi by her Sikh bodyguards after Indian troops stormed the Golden Temple in Amritsar to quell Sikh militants pressing for self-rule, as well as the 21 May 1991 assassination of Rajiv Gandhi by a Tamil suicide bomber. Both cases were accompanied by communal violence which, in 1984, for example, was facilitated by officials from the ruling Indian National Congress.

In 1992, India witnessed a major outbreak of Hindu–Muslim violence after the destruction of Babri Masjid at Ayodhya by Hindu nationalists, which led to over 1,200 deaths. In 2002, when BJP's Narendra Modi was the chief minister of Gujarat, widespread Hindu–Muslim violence erupted in Gujarat after a train carrying Hindu pilgrims returning from Ayodhya was attacked by a Muslim mob. Resulting in thousands of deaths, the unrest was the worst since Partition.

While the threat of communalism and militancy has proliferated since Independence, the underlying nature of Indian politics has also evolved, potentially altering its secular origins. After the 1975–7 Emergency, during which the democratic process was suspended, the make-up of India's political landscape began to shift as Congress, on occasions, also inculcated mass politics and populism, and invoked religious identity into the campaigning of elections in the 1980s.

Such actions appeared to weaken the tolerant, plural, and secular nature of Indian democracy, as principally promoted by Congress and Nehru, and led to an increase in explicitly communal and lower-caste politics in the late 1980s and 1990s. In parallel, electoral and communal violence also became a normalized feature of politics during this period. Such developments underpin how secularism in India is in many ways continually contested, and affected by communalist pressures. Furthermore, all political entities are interacting within the same political spectrum and tensions.

The emergence of the Hindu nationalist BJP, whose Hindutva philosophy and majoritarian focus openly countered Congress's secularism, appeared to substantially contest the secular character of the Indian state. In 1998, the BJP-led National Democratic Alliance (NDA) coalition assumed power, becoming the first such non-Congress entity to achieve power in modern Indian history—apart from the rainbow Janata coalition that briefly held power after the 1975–7 Emergency. This event confirmed the ascendancy of political tendencies within India that challenged the core nature and primary principles of her democratic topography that had been in place since 1947.

The 1998–2004 NDA revealed clear dissonances in the political approaches of the BJP and Congress, with the latter's belief in equality, tolerance, secularism, and plurality confronted by the latter's cultural nationalism and positive secularism, which were both Hindu–dominated. Positive secularism contrasted to Congress's form of secularism, which was seen as pseudo-secular and, according to the BJP, discriminated against the rights of the majority Hindu population of India. While these sentiments characterized the different political ideologies underpinning each grouping, and thus personified their periods in office—rather than deeper, longer lasting developments—the ascendancy of the BJP to power ended Congress's near monopoly on power since the Nehru era.

From this basis, the foundational understandings in regard to Indian democracy and secularism evolved, acknowledging, and in effect learning from these alternative values and principles. As such, the largely socialist leaning of India's political system became more multifaceted and composite in nature, as the BJP was established as a legitimate political force and governing alternative to Congress. In turn, because of their Hindu basis, the BJP's political presence and success also diluted anti-communal sentiments and legitimized the validity of communal politics, as personified by the BJP's active discrimination against Muslims, Christians, and the lower castes.

By being a successful communal grouping that was able to counter Congress's secular and inclusive heritage, the BJP's outright majority in the 2014 election accelerated this change. While highlighting an ongoing tension between the two entities, the BJP's electoral success continues to normalize their world view and has shifted the centre ground of Indian politics towards their ideas, lastingly altering the political landscape. The BJP's wide support among India's emergent middle class, who benefit from continued neoliberal economic growth, bolsters this progression.

Even though communal tendencies are now mainstreamed into India's political basis, seemingly defying its secular essence, they still have the potential to cause tensions and instabilities. At the most basic level, these can unsettle India's political underpinnings. For these reasons, communal violence between any of India's manifold religious, ethnic, social, and political identities—even paradoxically including the BJP and the Indian National Congress—remains feasible. This is a threat to her democratic foundations and the overall principle of secularism enshrined since Independence. In turn, myriad separatist and insurgent groups continue to majorly threaten India's democratic basis through their efforts to establish rival forms of political organization.

Sovereignty and Territory

The second major set of national security interests in the Indian context relate to the maintenance of her sovereign and territorial integrity. In a similar manner to the underlying foundations and essence structuring the last domain, the influence of history and its recollection is highly apparent, especially the impact of colonial Britain's ruling principles. Moreover, elements of national control, self-sufficiency, and autonomy all remain actively present today.

Within South Asia, India's new leaders continued the legacy of the British Raj's emphasis on utilizing a centralized administration whereby the ruling government dominated the provinces. Confirming this stance, India's Constitution comprises specific national security tools designed to enable the reassertion of central control, via the enactment of emergency powers through what is known as President's Rule, whereby the prime minister can subject all national functions to direct rule (Articles 356 and 357). Such Articles act as an institutionalized reaction to any threats against India's secular and unified political basis, as well as any potential threats to her territorial integrity.

President's Rule has been used against individual states on at least 120 occasions (especially in Kashmir), as well as during the 1962 war with China and the 1971 liberation of East Pakistan. The most extreme version of such powers, that is, Article 352, allows for the proclamation of an emergency 'whereby the security of India or of any part of the territory thereof is threatened, whether by war or external aggression or armed rebellion'. This Article was invoked by Indira Gandhi in 1975 and led to the legislature and the Constitution being suspended, the use of press censorship, the detention of politicians and protestors, and many political groups being banned.

Independence also bought with it a range of territorial disputes that threatened the ideal geographical image of India. Apart from the unclear Curzon and

McMahon lines demarcating her northern borders with China, Nepal, and Bhutan, the Mountbatten Plan precipitated Partition that attempted to split the country into contiguous Hindu- and Muslim-dominated areas. This division was accompanied by a number of territorial ambiguities, most notably that the new Pakistan was split into two separate wings, more than 1,600 kilometres apart.

Other territorial problems also typified the Mountbatten Plan. Some of these were solved quickly, such as the absorption of Junagadh and Hyderabad in 1947 and 1948, respectively, aided by the Indian military. On the other hand, Jammu and Kashmir, whose leader Hari Singh wished for the state to become independent in 1947, was virulently contested by both India and Pakistan, who would then periodically wage wars (primarily in 1947–8, 1965, and 1999) over its possession.

Regarded as symbolic of their national identities— but which are juxtaposed with each other—holding onto Kashmir became a strategic imperative for both India and Pakistan. Ideologically non-negotiable, existential, and zero sum, both sides feared the demonstration effect of Kashmir seceding to the other as it would question the basis of their relative sovereignties. Kashmir came to signify threats to the legitimacy of the new India, both in terms of her physical make-up and her political values, personifying much more than simply land. Such sentiments would become entrenched through conflict with Pakistan and insurgency emanating from the region, making Kashmir's reacquisition a non-contestable issue with India. Central to both their national security interests, and thus a mutual threat, Kashmir's status hence became intractable.

Although not yet successful in Kashmir, an ongoing campaign of territorial consolidation has been carried out by India that stresses the importance of geography and territory as properties of her sovereignty. Thus, New Delhi has taken back enclaves formerly claimed by foreign powers, including Pondicherry from France (via a 1954 agreement that came to fruition in 1962), Goa in 1961 from Portugal (via military force), and the reabsorption of Sikkim in 1975. Indicating an ideal sense of her geographical extent, and an underlying opposition to territorial expansion and conquest as a national security tool, in 1951 India returned one of the Coco Islands to Myanmar.

India also faces another large territorial dispute on her northern borders with China, which again is indicative of how an apparently internal national security issue (a country's self-ascribed territorial extent) necessarily blurs into foreign affairs through contested borders. Dating from their 1962 conflict, which India heavily lost, China has laid claim to over 90,000 square kilometres of Arunachal Pradesh. As another tangible, and long-standing, threat to her sovereignty, in 1963—as part of their own ever-close strategic relations—China was also ceded a portion of Pakistan-controlled Kashmir (the Shasgam Valley) by Islamabad and further controls 38,000 square kilometres of nearby Aksai Chin, also within the sphere of Kashmir's territory. India's 1962 defeat would spur on increased spending on her military as a national security tool.

Apart from exemplifying specific threats to one of her particular national interests, these three out-standing territorial disputes with Pakistan and China concurrently raise ongoing reservations concerning the intentions of Islamabad and Beijing towards New Delhi. Such suspicions, in many ways acting as proto-fears, serve as constant touchstones in these bilateral relations, underscoring the role of perceptions in their specific interactional and dynamic self/other dyads. As with Pakistan, such distrust has contributed to border skirmishes between India and China, most notably at Nathula in 1967, at Somdurong Chu in 1987, and many more in recent years.

Pertaining to Britain's previous desire for influence and supremacy across South Asia, India also inherited a Curzonian mindset concerning her wider position in the region. This mindset involved stretching her authority downwards into the entire Indian Ocean region from Singapore to Aden. Control of the ocean rested upon historical experience whereby British, Dutch, and French colonialists had all assaulted India from the sea, underlining its criticality as being 'India's Lake'. At the same time, the domination over her smaller neighbours—Bangladesh, Bhutan, Nepal, and Sri Lanka—was intended to prevent them from being used by external actors (including countries but also insurgents and militants) as bases from which India's territory could be threatened, and which, by extension, ensured her continued internal stability.

Unequal security treaties thus typified these relations, such as the 1950 Treaty of Peace and Friendship with Nepal whose Article 5 made it compulsory for Kathmandu to tell New Delhi of any planned arms purchases, and effectively allowed India to co-opt and control her national security direction. At the same time, India's military forces have been used as a deterrent and as an interventionist force in the region, engaging in bilateral peacemaking operations in Nepal (1950), Sri Lanka (1971 and 1987–90), and the Maldives (1988). Such actions asserting regional control again allowed India to bolster her national security by aiding the stability of her borders, and by extension her sovereignty and the various internal values upon which it is based. Notably, New Delhi still has outstanding border disputes with many of these smaller countries.

While now less assertive than the 1970s Indira Doctrine, that was explicitly and draconically geared to prevent countries in the region having any relations with external actors that could be seen as anti-Indian, New Delhi's dominance has been perpetuated primarily through economic diplomacy. With the same national security interests at heart, that is to maintain control and stability, these mechanisms—such as the reciprocal 1990s Gujral Doctrine—also play a long-term role concerning meeting India's energy security needs through the supply of hydropower, oil, and gas.

In all these ways, the use of such diplomacy acts as a critical means to bind other countries together with India, create interdependence, and potentially reduce the occurrence of instability. It also helps confront other threats to a country's territorial integrity, including the smuggling and trafficking of currency, people, drugs, and wildlife. Establishing closer relations based upon other initiatives concerning finance, education, energy, disaster management, and pandemics, are also diplomatic tools that enhance national security through the pursuit of international relations.

Modernization and Great Power

Our final domain for consideration displays both tangible and aspirational elements within the expanse of

India's national security interests. Concerning the former part, modernizing and developing the country has been a critical aim for all of India's political factions, acting as a test of their legitimacy to represent and protect its citizens as elected leaders of the sovereign state. Ensuring India's energy, water, and food security fall within the remit of the wider policy since the 1990s of maintaining the high rates of economic growth essential to achieving these aims.

Interlinked, and also serving as their logical extension, Indian leaders have simultaneously sought to use economic growth to enhance their country's overall international stature. In particular, the convertibility of economic prowess to other kinds of power, such as military, diplomatic, and so on, not only increases India's comprehensive national power vis-à-vis her neighbouring countries and other large powers on the international stage but also fundamentally enhances her national security. In these ways, amassing such power can be used to amalgamate efforts to protect major security interests such as her sovereignty and borders, political system, and societal consistency.

From this basis, the pursuit of an ambition to be a great power is, therefore, as much a national security interest as is protection against a specific fear. In addition, if and when India's status—either in its actual or desired state—is menaced, it also becomes an existential threat to this self-image and henceforth her national security. For her elites, the aspiration to become a great power originated in the perceived historical significance of earlier Indian empires, as well as her various conquests by external powers, especially by Britain, that reaffirmed her importance. Once such recognition is attained, so too will the virtue of purna swaraj, thus ensuring her survival.

Within this paradigm, India's external global behaviour has sought to ensure her national security aims. Thus, New Delhi's policy of non-alignment, for instance, can be regarded as an international realization of her specific domestic values. Concurrently, casting the country as being outside the bipolarity of the Cold War, non-alignment generated India moral and diplomatic legitimacy and influence, even if she was materially weak and impoverished. It also enabled the promotion of core principles like anti-imperialism, anti-colonialism, and peaceful development.

By then, gaining a greater voice in international affairs via the establishment of the Non-Aligned Movement, India acquired the means to both pro-tect and promote her national interests, particularly in the earliest years after Independence when her very existence was under scrutiny. Crucially, non-alignment indicated a form of active neutrality rather than isolationism. Other key principles interplayed with non-alignment, including non-intervention and non-aggression, which counteracted high military spending, at least prior to 1962. Both of these allowed India's domestic development by creating a less threatening, and peaceful and stable external environment.

Regarding India's domestic modernization and development, economic self-reliance (swadeshi) was the mainstay of the initial approach taken by elites in New Delhi. Emphasizing socialist self-sufficiency and self-reliance, swadeshi rested upon privileging domestic production and limiting international engagement, including foreign involvement and investment. This method intended to discourage external influences, whereby the state was the key inculcator of economic growth, and was thoroughly symptomatic of her post-colonial suspicion of the international system. We can also recall that pre-1947 imperial invaders had systematically taken India's wealth and status. The swadeshi approach was thus suited to developing the country's fragile infrastructure.

Despite some mild attempts at reform from the mid-1960s onwards, it was only in the 1990s—the time when India experienced a serious balance-of-payments crisis—that a full-fledged programme for economic liberalization as per prevailing international practices was undertaken. India's declining industrial and economic support from the Soviet Union—New

Delhi's then most important ally—after its collapse after the end of the Cold War also spurred on the reforms. This development underlines how wider changes in the global structure can alter the means taken to achieve a country's national security interests. Emblematic of such maturation, India was now forced to see the benefits, not the demerits, of liberalization and globalization for her national modernization. Such benefits related as much to her domestic values as they did to her internal development, and were alternative means to achieve self-reliance, autonomy, and great power.

In the aftermath of the 1962 war with China, however, such sentiments were yet to be realized, as the defeat revealed the susceptibility of her non-aligned and peaceful principles, in particular New Delhi's low military spending which had facilitated India's defeat. Resulting in enhanced levels of expenditure, the war socialized India into the practices of the international order, and showed us elements of learning and adaptation whereby lessons from negative experiences were used to redirect policy priorities and preferences. Without necessarily diminishing her core national security interests, it was again the means to achieve and safeguard such interests that were altered. As such, an insistence on moral principles was supplemented by acquiring material means.

India's 1965 victory against Pakistan strengthened the country's self-sufficiency. As also her 1971 liberation of East Pakistan, which eased the two threats previously posed by Islamabad, and involved New Delhi's judicious use of treaty diplomacy with the Soviet Union prior to the conflict to balance out Pakistan's links with China. These events increased India's regional standing along with the general stability of the region, and effectively established her as South Asia's most influential state with the capacity to redefine her strategic environment. Such events were important to enabling her continued internal development, as well as heightening her overall status, as aided by her acquisition of nuclear capabilities via the 1974 Peaceful Nuclear Explosion.

As the 1980s and 1990s progressed, the scope of India's external interaction and affairs increased, driven by the dual spurs of heightening her economic growth and augmenting her global standing. This expansion encompassed looking beyond the confines of South Asia to improve and balance her diplomatic relations in West Asia (especially between the Arab states and Israel) and South East Asia (in particular with the military junta in Myanmar). West Asia's growing importance to India concerning the supply of oil and gas made it a key area in her energy security, as did ensuring continued remittances from Indian workers, especially from the Gulf states. Ties with Central Asia and Iran also increased and centred upon energy and trade exchanges.

Within these often-circular dynamics, whereby expanding economic growth requires more energy supplies which leads to more economic development that demands ever-greater energy provision, the bandwidth of India's engagement increased as did the repertoire of her diplomacy. Within these burgeoning interactions, India's external affairs became more and more complicated, thus pulling more influences, issues, and concerns into the sphere of her national security interests. As their interconnection has increased, foreign policy became more essential to the national interest.

Within the scope of trade and energy security, for example, enhanced imports and exports now demand India's commitment to ensure the safety of the supply of oil, gas, and other commodities to her major industries. They also mean protecting associated overseas workers, building up appropriate protective naval capabilities, and being involved in bilateral treaties and multilateral organizations. As her economic growth increases relative to others, India also has to be involved in talks on global financial practices, and on dealing with unwanted effects like global warming. Ever blossoming in scope, such interactions thus indicate exponential national security interests.

Within all of these perspectives, India's approach to national security slowly eschewed Nehruvian idealism and embraced level-headed pragmatism as the best means to pursue its interests. Indian policymakers became more assertive and confident, professing India to be a global power. Closer ties with the United States from the early 1990s onwards are telling in this regard, and reversed decades of animosity and suspicion between the two sides. These relations have been central to increasing India's global standing, as well as facilitating access to global capitalism, which New Delhi now sought to actively foster rather than reject as per the workings of swadeshi.

Critical Influences

Just as different counties will have competing visions concerning what represents their national security interests, within countries there will also be a plurality of opinion concerning them. Thus, whilst the core national security interests in the three primary domains of India's national security remain constant, the understandings shaping them are open to debate, as are the very means deployed to combat specific threats and fears, and to fulfil particular desires or ambitions.

The values and culture exemplifying India's major political groups act as the clearest areas of divergence, principally between the Indian National Congress and the BJP. Producing a different emphasis, style, and approach to national security, how these parties have governed India affects the very way in which threats, and the responses to deal with them, are conceived. Therefore, as Katzenstein remarks, '[H]istory is a process of change that leaves an imprint on state identity' (Katzenstein 1996).

Competing conceptions of the world has resulted in the specific political orientations, policies, and practices of these parties. As such, Congress ostensibly rests upon principles of equality, plurality, and tolerance, so as to engender a secular and inclusive India as part of a socialist and anti-communal democracy. Most Congress leaders have held to these values, notwithstanding the use of majoritarian politics by some of their leaders in the 1980s. In comparison, the BJP's Hindutva vision is typified by cultural superiority, a distrust of outsiders (mostly Muslims and Christians), and a desire to make India into a *Hindu rashtra* (Hindu country), which pursues 'cultural nationalism' as a unifying code to realize a Hindu-dominated world view. Concerning economics, the BJP promotes a much more pro-capitalist version of Congress's socialist swadeshi that is more centred upon Hindu nationalism and India's soon-to-be great power pre-eminence.

Besides the influence of these major political group-ings, and the wider patronage networks within which they are based, various other domestic actors, be they the public at large, figures from the worlds of media, business and academia, or the Indian diaspora, are all having an ever greater influence upon national security debates. Together with retired bureaucrats and officials from government ministries and the armed services, who often take up positions at many of India's increas-ing number of think tanks, such actors collectively represent India's security community.

The proliferation of India's print, visual, and digital media from the 1990s onwards has in turn augmented the means by which key debates concerning national security, and, by its logical extension, foreign policy, are able to connect the wider Indian population with news sources and opinion. The widespread use of English boosts these interactions, as does an expanding middle class that is increasingly well-educated, vocal, and invested in continued economic growth. Across the third of our domains (modernization and great power), the interplay between domestic development demands and a necessarily evocative foreign policy is ever more evident.

As a result, India's leaders and policymakers can-not ignore these domestic constituencies as virulent, demanding, and highly nationalistic forces. These elements are also particularly present online, especially via the brisk expansion in the use of social media, with some three quarters and one half of India's population being mobile phone and Internet users, respectively, in 2016. When mixed with the persistence of communal tendencies, such nationalism acts as a volatile variable, especially within a population experiencing rapid economic and societal transformations. As such, it majorly influences national security, most acutely when mixed with electoral politics.

Finally, we must consider that the environment in which India now operates on the international scale is also changing and evolving, no more so than New Delhi's slow embrace of globalization. Opening up the country to liberal, market-led economics is an unsettling experience for many Indians, and thus Indian nationalism also comprises an anti-corporate sentiment dating from the colonial period. Customarily anti-western and anti-US in nature, external stimuli are seen to threaten India's native values, culture, and identities, attitudes growing with her economic ascent.

India's National Interests

Our delineation of the three principle domains highlight the national interests central to India's national security. Within each of them, the overarching inter-est—democracy and secularism; sovereignty and territory; and modernization and great power—is characterized by a set of specific national security issues which are indicative of certain threats or fears to that interest. It is these threats that the Indian govern-ment and leaders must specifically protect the coun-try against. This interrelated and dynamic interaction highlights not only a complex phenomenon but also that the essential function of national security is to protect the national interests of a country.

In the first domain, threats take the form of any groups that seek to promote any alternative form of organization that opposes the core national values essential to Indian democracy. By extension, these thus endanger the foundational values of inclusiveness, unity, and tolerance. The major threats in this regard are militancy, separatism, and communalism, which personify the central fear of Indian society destabilizing and breaking up, leading to the country's dissolution.

For the second domain, threats to India's physical extent necessarily concern her neighbouring states whose own self-conceptions as per their territorial nature frequently clash and overlap with India's. Most pertinently these relate to Pakistani claims in Kashmir, and Chinese assertions in Arunachal Pradesh and Aksai Chin, plus some other smaller disputes. Again, they exemplify fears concerning the strength of India's national integrity and her prospective balkanization.

Regarding the third domain, the threats to India's perceived standing as a modern, developed, and important global entity are those that potentially retard or slow down such a desired trajectory. Myriad concerns permeate this domain, including the energy and trade security needed to fuel her economic rise, alongside the diplomatic influence required to pursue her goals globally. At the heart of this domain, the central fear is that of India's destiny being not fulfilled which will not thus only impact on her status but also impede her self-sufficiency and autonomy in the world.

All of these interests, and related threats or fears, underscore the interconnected nature of security. They also confirm how socially constructed understandings act as the means by which countries fear and desire particular outcomes. In these ways, we have seen how history, identity, culture, and perceptions, of India and others, underpin, embolden, and build these perspectives, whereby the past acts as a repository for understanding both present and future interactions.

2

India's Internal Aspects

In this chapter we investigate the internal dimensions of Indian national security. Attention is given to the bureaucratic and governmental institutions concerned with national security, such as intelligence, police, and border agencies, as well as the role of the army and a discussion on relevant legislation, infrastructure, and emergency measures. These are all critical tools with which India's leaders can further national security aims and interests against specific threats and internal as well as external actors. This book's key themes of history, identity, culture, and perception remain evident, highlighting the presence of an India-specific national security that is interacting across internal and external spheres, and which is characterized by being self-reinforcing and gestating in nature.

Providing internal stability and coherence, primarily via protection of the Indian landmass, has become a major element of New Delhi's national security remit. Within such dynamics, the enduring significance of domestic threats such as separatism (including the Kashmir and Arunachal Pradesh issues), insurgency, and terrorism are evident. These matters are further manifest concerning policy towards Punjab and the North-East, along with the threat posed by Naxalites and others. The internal dimension also includes more non-military and developmental security concerns, mainly in relation to poverty, human rights, corruption, pollution (including degradation and disaster relief), as well as growing demographic pressures and social inequalities.

National security at its most basic level means survival—of a country, its sovereignty, and its peoples—with leaders and elites being responsible for meeting the needs inherent to this aim. Of note is that our three domains—democracy and secularism, sovereignty and territory, and modernization and great power—map onto elements within Maslow's hierarchy of needs. At the bottom of this hierarchy are biological and physiological needs, such as access to food, water, warmth, and shelter. Above these come safety needs, including security (of body, employment, resources, family, health, and property), law and order, stability, and freedom from fear. Beyond these then are esteem needs of independence, status, dominance, prestige, and respect from others, and at the hierarchy's apex, self-actualization needs in terms of realizing potential and self-fulfilment. Together, these needs effectively sum up the major domains of India's national security concerns.

Institutions and Legislation

A range of bureaucratic and governmental institutions, and their accompanying major agencies and legal provisions, provide India's most potent national security tools. At the fulcrum, and emblematic of a highly leader-centric system symptomatic of Nehru's dominance over security planning, coordination, and implementation, lies the Prime Minister's Office (PMO). Formally institutionalized by Lal Bahadur Shastri, the PMO acts as the managing body of all the Indian ministries and enshrines the position of the prime minister as the head of the Indian executive. As per constructivism, this body thus enshrines an institutional and governmental culture wherein the prime minister has been historically preponderant concerning national security. The PMO takes advice on national security matters from a range of government ministries and major institutions, as shown in Figure 2.1, along with specific policy advisors and civil servants.

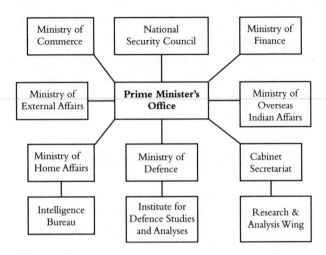

FIGURE 2.1 Governmental and Institutional Influences upon the PMO

Source: Ogden (2014b: 21).

The major ministries reporting directly to the PMO cover the full range of internal and external aspects of national security (along with matters further relating to foreign policy). Hence, internal security provision broadly falls under the aegis of the Ministry of Home Affairs (MoHA), including India's domestic policing requirements. International relations (including dealing with neighbouring states, as is key to border security) fall under the Ministry of External Affairs (MEA). As per our core analytical domains, the ministries of

Finance and Commerce also feature as they encompass economic and energy security concerns and provide the funding of national security arrangements. The centrality of these ministries has been evident since Independence and, by maintaining their historical and contemporary significance, they are now an engrained aspect of India's institutional identity.

Beyond these entities, the Ministry of Defence features due to India's armed forces being the primary overt tool with which to manage, alleviate, and counter national security threats. Focus is also given to representing the interests of Indians abroad through the MEA, and this is another example of how national security interests often necessitate a global angle. Finally, we can also observe the presence of India's intelligence services; the Intelligence Bureau (IB), India's internal intelligence agency and the Research and Analysis Wing (R&AW), India's external intelligence agency, both of which are discussed in detail subsequently.

Acting as a condensed version of the expertise filtering into the PMO, India's supreme national security body is the National Security Council (NSC). Formally consecrated by the BJP-led NDA government during its 1998–2004 rule, the NSC centralizes and oversees the running of India's security policy. A small group of ministers from the most crucial departments constitute the NSC, along with the national security adviser who is the chief executive of the NSC and acts as the prime minister's key security confidante. Its structure can be seen in Figure 2.2. Acting as a highly focused power base in terms of their national roles, responsibilities, and remits, the importance of these individuals to the delineation of India's national security is paramount, and it again reflects the historical importance of such positions and their specific security interests.

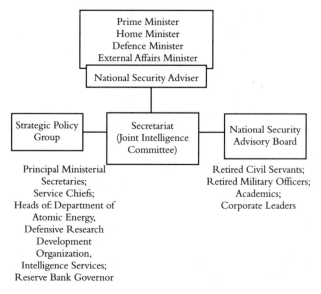

FIGURE 2.2   India's National Security Council

Source: Ogden (2014b: 22).

Displaying a greater degree of focus compared with the PMO, various bodies concerning the complete range of national security matters report to these core leaders or ministers. These are the Strategic Policy Group, which undertakes periodic Strategic Defence Reviews of short- and long-term security threats; the Joint Intelligence Committee, which analyses intelligence data from the IB, the R&AW, and all of India's armed forces, and the National Security Advisory Board (NSAB), which consists of non-government experts (hand-picked by the prime minister), meets monthly (or more frequently, if required) and provides long-term prognosis and analysis.

India's domestic intelligence agency, the IB, was inherited from the British colonial period, further confirming the link between India's history/culture and its present-day identity. It is tasked with collecting intelligence, concerning any threats to India's national security, and carrying out counter-intelligence (especially counter-terrorism) activities. These undertakings involve the interception and monitoring of physical and electronic communications, and agents received training from the KGB prior to the collapse of the Soviet Union at the end of the 1980s. As with any domestic security services, the scope of most of IB operations remains highly classified.

The IB held responsibility for both internal and external security but after the disastrous war with China in 1962, and some intelligence failings surrounding the 1965 conflict with Pakistan, a separate external agency was created in September 1968—the R&AW. The R&AW's initial remit focused on monitoring China and Pakistan as those of India's neighbours most likely to have a deliberatively negative impact on its national security. The R&AW was also instrumental in training freedom fighters who helped presage the liberation of East Pakistan in 1971 (which led to the formation of Bangladesh), and trained Tamil separatists in Sri Lanka in the 1970s and 1980s.

More broadly, the R&AW's core objective is to carry out covert operations abroad in order to protect India's national security interests. This concerns the collection of information relating to military, political, economic, and scientific intelligence through both covert and overt means, primarily via espionage, surveillance, and subversion, as well as via sabotage and assassination. Their remit also includes a focus upon the smuggling of any arms, explosives, and ammunition into India that could be potentially used by state or non-state sponsored actors. Bolstering these capabilities, it exchanges information with a number of other security agencies, most notably the CIA in the US, MI6 in the UK, Israel's Mossad, as well as the FSB in Russia. Such interaction influences India's national security identity, interests, and threat perceptions.

Beyond the IB and R&AW is a plethora of other intelligence agencies in India, which provides further specializations concerning information gathering and analysis. These include from India's armed services, either collectively (via the Defence Intelligence Agency, set up in 2002, and the Signals Intelligence Directorate) or individual branches (such as the Directorate of Air Intelligence and the Directorate of Naval Intelligence). Specific agencies relating to drug smuggling, tax evasion, and corruption (principally the Narcotics Control Bureau, the Directorate of Revenue Intelligence, and the Directorate of Income Tax) are also in place, and these can be seen as adjunct areas that affect—if rather more marginal—aspects of India's national security.

Most powerful, especially in the contemporary climate of interconnected globalization, is the Joint Cypher Bureau, responsible for cryptanalysis and encryption for India's armed services. There is also the National Technical Research Organization that gathers technical intelligence and then channels it to other agencies concerned with internal and external security. This involves satellite, terrestrial, and Internet monitoring relating to India's border, maritime, and land security. The Central Bureau of Investigation (CBI) also deals with crimes against the national economy, including fraud and embezzlement, while state-level police forces deal with all other offences. Thus, in their own ways, these bodies are all tools with which to improve India's national security.

The most potent means of intelligence gathering is the Central Monitoring System, which allows for the direct surveillance or interception of all mobile (and landline) phones and as Internet communications within India. Underscoring its prowess, telecom operators are required by law to provide data access to all of the intelligence agencies or law enforcement detailed above. Specific warrants are not required concerning its usage, leading to criticism relating to the dilution of individual privacy and rights of Indian citizens; a lack of clear oversight, transparency, checks and balances that may lead to its conceivable abuse; as well as it being a tool of state authoritarianism. In conjunction with her myriad intelligence groupings, the potency of this system confirms a historically rooted fear of instability that is central to India's national security identity and culture.

The supremacy of these various agencies and groupings is buoyed by the Indian Constitution, which contains several provisions designed to protect India's national security basis. In many ways mimicking British colonial legislation, Article 352 allows for the declaration of a national emergency in response to any grave threat to Indian security or territory resulting from war, external aggression, or internal disturbance (or its imminent realization). Giving the central government a range of powers, these include the suspension of Article 19 of the Constitution that provides vital rights to her citizens, as well as giving it control over the affairs of all states.

Between 1950 and 1975, Article 352 was enacted twice in 1962 and 1971, at the time of war with China and with Pakistan. This was accompanied by the granting of sweeping powers to the executive, including the 1962 Defence of India Act that allowed for preventative detention. The powers under Article 352 also allowed for restrictions on freedom of movement, freedom of assembly, broad warrantless search and seizure powers, and the suspension of many judicial procedures. In both cases, the emergency powers were maintained into peacetime, with the 1962 enactment extending until 1968, and in 1971 until 1977 (encompassing Indira Gandhi's 1975–7 Emergency). As a result, India has been under emergency rule for over 11 years of her modern existence.

In reaction to the 1975–7 Emergency—when India's democratic process was suspended, over 110,000 individuals were detained, press freedom was curtailed, and judicial powers were diminished—the successor Janata coalition amended the Constitution. Aimed at preventing a repeat of 1975–7, the grounds of 'internal disturbance' were replaced with 'armed rebellion', while the automatic suspension of rights relating to freedom of speech, expression, association, and assembly was no longer permissible. Article 352, however, remains in place and it is the most forceful legal provision concerning national security available to any Indian leader, along with President's Rule whereby the prime minister can subject all state/national functions to direct rule (via Articles 356 and 357).

Specific legislation is also in place to allow India's elites, governments, and bureaucracies to assert legal measures intended to defend aspects of national security. The most longstanding of these are the various Armed Forces (Special Powers) Acts that have been granted to give India's armed forces extraordinary authority in what are considered to be 'disturbed areas'. These have been enacted in 1958 (concerning Assam and Manipur, but then across all of India's seven North-Eastern states), in 1983 (in Punjab and Chandigarh), and in 1990 (in Jammu and Kashmir). Each of them remain in place, except for the 1983 Act, and provide armed forces with emergency powers including extra-legal clout that seemingly suspend various human rights and judicial procedures.

Outside of these state-specific and situation-specific legal provisions, there is the Unlawful Activities (Prevention) Act of 1967, which criminalizes association or support of any domestic or external organization that 'disclaims, questions, disrupts, or is intended to disrupt the sovereignty or territorial integrity of India'. The Act is specifically targeted against separatist, insurgent, and terrorist groupings and, in 2016, there were over 35 consortia that were prescribed under its remit. Taken all together, this range of legislation shows us how a need for control, and the inverse fear of instability, has been present in India from the colonial period to the present day. Such a persistent perception has become part of New Delhi's national security culture and, through their India-specific orientation, a part of her identity as per our constructivist theoretical framework.

Following different manifestations, other legislation provides a legal structure and apparatus for the principles, aims, and interests of Indian national security to be ostensibly protected—as per the three domains underpinning its guiding essences as derived from historical experience. These include the general National Security Act of 1980 and the Terrorism and Disruptive Activities (Prevention) Act of 1987 (known as TADA) intended to enable internal stability. Building on TADA's existing anti-terrorist provisions, the draconian Prevention of Terrorism Act (POTA; akin to its precursor, the 2001 Prevention of Terrorism Ordinance) was introduced in 2002.

Due to widespread criticism that POTA variously allowed security forces to hold individuals for up to 180 days without charge, expanded the reach of the death penalty, denied any presumption of innocence, granted officials immunity, and allowed confession through torture, the Act was repealed in 2004 despite some political opposition. Legal provision now rests on the Unlawful Activities (Prevention) Act, which has been amended on multiple occasions to include more measures designed to combat threats to national security, plus the ongoing National Security Act. Such amendments point to the ongoing evolution and gestation of India's national security outlook. More recently, the National Investigation Agency Bill of 2008 also sanctioned extensive legal powers that are pre-meditated 'to constitute an investigation agency at the national level to investigate and prosecute offences affecting the sovereignty, security and integrity of India'.

Finally, to these we can add the anti-sedition Section 124A of the Indian Penal Code of 1870, which is devised to counter 'whoever, by words, either spoken or written, or by signs, or by visible representation, or otherwise, brings or attempts to bring into hatred or contempt, or excites or attempts to excite disaffection towards the Government'. Section 124A is regarded as highly controversial due its vast potential scope, which remains heavily dependent upon whatever interpretations/criteria whichever elite actor chooses to use when deciding to authorize its use. Again, this points to the criticality of perceptions concerning what is meant by national security.

Besides the escalating military capabilities (as will be discussed in Chapter 3), the Indian Constitution mandates that the responsibility for law and order rests with individual states and territories, resulting in a number of police forces controlled by a state's chief minister and home minister. Forming both unarmed and armed contingents, the latter—often referred to as paramilitaries—is used to manage public events, to respond to incidences of unrest and communal rioting, and to combat criminal activities. Most states also have anti-terrorism squads and intelligence apparatus. With responsibility for the security concerns, interests, and fears of specific states, such groupings will all be influenced by—and also influence—India's country-level national security behaviour.

In addition, there is the Central Armed Police Services under the control of the MoHA. Encompassing a number of groupings amounting to 1.3 million paramilitaries, it includes the Central Reserve Police Force, which assists state-level policing; the Border

Security Force, the Indo-Tibetan Border Police, and the Sashastra Seema Bal—which collectively guard India's borders and target the smuggling of drugs, guns, people, and fake currency—and the Central Industrial Security Force that protects vital government infrastructure and installations (including ports, oil refineries, and power plants). To these can be added the National Security Guards, an elite counter-terrorism commando unit; the Special Protection Group designated to protect past and present prime ministers and other elites; and the Indian Home Guard and Civil Defence. Other informal paramilitary units are also regularly activated across many of India's states, often in response to specific security issues.

Beyond these governance and legal arrangements, there are some other groupings concerning national security, which are of note, principally in terms of their influence (or lack thereof). First, although national security rests with the PMO and NSC, the Indian Parliament remains as a key source of deliberation, stimulus, and guidance. Although restricted, it debates on major issues impacting upon the direction and tenor of national security, votes on annual budgets, represents the concerns or interests of their constituents and, via Standing Committees, scrutinizes annual reports, and can summon or cross-examine officials. All of these processes inject greater levels of (albeit often limited) inspection, accountability, and consultation. They also confirm the significance of internal interaction in the construction of national security.

Furthermore, the MEA, through its historical knowledge, experience, and concern with India's wider regional and international environment, is also an important factor. Responsible for the implementation of foreign policy, its diplomatic engagement on a bilateral and multilateral basis concerning myriad military, economic, and political affairs is necessarily a reflection of India's national security interests. The MEA's External Publicity Division is critical regarding media diplomacy in the current information-laden era, so as to manage India's international image and to help propagate, publicize, and ultimately achieve her national security objectives. The MEA's institutional memory is another input into India's national security identity and outlook.

In turn, it is notable that in terms of direct decision-making the military plays a marginal role in the national security process. This distancing reflects the non-politicized nature of India's bureaucracy and police services as a whole, along with predominantly non-aggressive principles towards security (at least initially espoused by Nehru and Mahatma Gandhi). Such a longstanding culture traditionally insisted that the military has a subordinate function. Influence may be growing, however, in the context of India's overall modernization process, especially concerning budgeting vis-à-vis the protection of maritime trade and energy security routes. Many think tanks are also manned by retired military officials, who do have an impact on the wider national security debates, as do various vocal academics, business leaders, media commentators, and the diaspora.

Internal Stability

This range of tools, as outlined, have been periodically deployed by India's major elites to counteract specific threats to the core facets or domains integral to the country's national security. Such threats primarily relate to maintaining the integrity of her sovereignty and territorial self-image, and also interweave with the wider domains of her core political values, as well as ongoing modernization goals en route to attaining the status of a great power in the international system. This interlinkage reveals how threats in one domain are tied to threats in other areas, and here concern the groups, entities, and other countries that menace the logic of India's physical nature. These dangers involve separatism, communalism, terrorism, and land dispute with neighbours.

Although one religious group dominates India's population (Hindus, at 80.5 per cent of the total), many others are also present. Besides Muslims (13.4 per cent), Christians (2.3 per cent), and Sikhs (1.9 per cent), there are numerous smaller religious denominations and groupings, which add complexity to the country's ethnic make-up, especially when multiplied by the fact that India's total population currently numbers over 1.3 billion. This intricacy is compounded by having at least 30 national and regional languages, and more than 2,000 dialects. Such elements point to a heterogeneous population, and raise the potential for destabilizing inter-communal tensions. The insistence of India's initial leaders upon secular principles is a countermeasure to such a factor.

The threat of domestic instability has been a longstanding and ongoing feature of India's internal security landscape, with New Delhi facing myriad sources of volatility emanating from within and without her borders. States in India's North-East (mainly Assam, Manipur, Nagaland, Tripura, and Mizoram) as well as states like Punjab and Jammu and Kashmir are the major founts of these threats, but there are also many other groupings that are functioning across India's more southern regions. As of early 2017, these threats included a total of 38 proscribed terrorist or external groups; 39 active terrorist, insurgent, or separatist groups; 121 inactive terrorist or insurgent groups, and 24 entities engaged in peace talks or ceasefires with the Indian government.

The well–established nature of these threats through the passage of history has built up a solid threat perception concerning the danger posed by all such groupings, and hence directly informs India's national security identity and culture as per this book's emphasis upon constructivism.

Many of these groups have historically and/or contemporarily received funding, training, shelter, or arms from India's neighbours—in particular Pakistan, China, Nepal, Bhutan, and Bangladesh. This is a factor which again extends a domestic/national security concern into the external/international sphere. The most conspicuous of these terrorist groups are currently the indigenous Indian Mujahideen, the Students Islamic Movement of India, Lashkar-e-Toiba (which carried out the Pakistan-sponsored November 2008 attacks in Mumbai), and Jaish-e-Mohammed—all of whom have orchestrated multiple bomb attacks across a number of Indian states during the last few decades.

Apart from such Muslim-focused groupings, there has also been evidence of Sikh- and Hindu-based terrorism (especially in the 1980s and 2000s, respectively), which was often linked to communal, ethnic, political, and criminal violence. Such violence has also resulted in frequent incidences of rioting, looting, arson, and bomb attacks. These frictions are longstanding, and date from the upheavals that accompanied India's Partition in 1947. Their repetition and recurrence has fully cemented such threats into the vast spectrum of India's core national security concerns, and again validates the role of history within the delineation of national security interests or fears.

Between 1994 and 2016, over 65,500 deaths (encompassing civilians, security forces, and terrorists) were attributed to these sources of violence and instability. This total includes 433 fatalities in 2016 alone, a significant decline from the peak of 5,839 deaths recorded in 2001. Most of these deaths occurred in Jammu and Kashmir, followed by Assam, Meghalaya, and Manipur. Although falling, such fatalities are still on a scale unrivalled by any other major international power, and are a consistent, gestating, and evolving form of threat to India's sovereign and territorial basis. Such a threat continues to justify and occupy her security forces. It also compounds the presence of such threats within India's national security identity, and can be regarded as a cultural security trait that has become engrained through history and interaction.

By far, the most powerful of the insurgent groupings active in India are the Naxalites. Formed in 1967 around a Maoist left-wing ideology, they largely represent indigenous tribal communities (Adivasis) and the lower castes with regard to land rights, unemployment, and the socio-economic exclusion. Active across at least a third of India's states, via the oft referred to 'red corridor' stretching from the north to the south of the country, the Naxalites caused over 7,300 deaths between 2005 and 2016. Although annual deaths are below their zenith of 1,180 in 2010, Naxalite activity accounted for nearly half of all such fatalities occurring across India in 2016.

In terms of the specific threat posed by the Naxalites, the group has been responsible for extensive assaults against police stations, army camps, state infrastructure (including bridges, roads, government buildings, and railway lines), private businesses (primarily iron ore mines and other heavy industries, oil pipelines, and tea plantations), as well as bank robberies, assassinations, kidnappings, and the bombing of trains, stations, and markets. For this reason, Manmohan Singh has referred to Naxalism as 'the single biggest internal security challenge ever faced by our country', with economic development regarded as the best way to counteract them. Perception and history thus play a major role in the Naxalites being an established threat in India.

Although innately concerning land and their commensurate national identities, India's dispute over

Jammu and Kashmir with neighbouring Pakistan has exhibited links with insurgency and terrorism—especially from the 1980s onwards. Pakistan-terrorism nexus has thus become a perceptible attribute within Indo-Pakistan relations, further broadening the scope of the Kashmir issue as a national security threat. In this regard, Pakistan supported separatist movements in Punjab from 1984 to 1992, and in Assam in the 1980s, while the Kashmir insurgency has itself inculcated Pakistani, Kashmiri, and Afghan militancy activity across India's North-Eastern states. The historically engrained persistence of such a threat makes it a key reference point within India's national security culture and identity, which has emerged by its interaction with Pakistan.

An assortment of terrorist acts has been linked to Pakistan, including the synchronized bomb attacks on Mumbai in 1993, and the protracted gun and bomb assault on the same city in November 2008. Pakistan's intelligence service, the Inter-Services Intelligence (ISI), has provided the material, financial, and logistic assistance for such attacks, as well as training facilities within its current portion of Jammu and Kashmir. Islamabad has also been linked to other events, such as the December 1999 hijacking of Indian Airlines Flight 814 by the Taliban, the 13 December 2001 attack on the Indian Parliament, as well as the funding of groups like Lashkar-e-Toiba.

Such activities are intended to not only secure Pakistan's eventual full possession of Jammu and Kashmir (hence threatening India's territorial and sovereign integrity) but also, on a wider scale, to destabilize India's internal cohesion. Fomenting separatist organizations falls within this logic, which aims to further weaken India's overall national unity and stability, and can thus potentially reduce New Delhi's military and economic dominance over South Asia. Other strategies have included attempts to disrupt the Indian stock market and to flood the Indian economy with counterfeit rupees. In the summer of 2012, Pakistan was also implicated in sending fake text messages so as to incite communal violence against Assamese workers in India's southern states. Competing identities thus form the fulcrum of the threat realities besetting Indo-Pak relations.

Jammu and Kashmir is not the only region of India that is currently contested by an external power. There is Arunachal Pradesh, which has been claimed by China since 1962 and is referred to as Southern Tibet by it, and there is also the Aksai Chin region in India's north-west. Again, these claims have the potential to delegitimize India's 'natural borders' and its physical self-image in the region. As such, they are major threats to her national security precepts concerning both her sovereignty and her territorial extent. Furthermore, they are also a threat to India's self-image and physical identity within South Asia. Amounting to 84,000 and 38,000 square kilometres respectively, Arunachal Pradesh and Aksai Chin represent 3.8 per cent of the Indian landmass, while Beijing also claims a small portion of Jammu and Kashmir (which itself overall 7.0 per cent).

Routine Chinese incursions across often inadequately distinguished borders continue to aggravate these territorial disputes, as do arguments that Beijing could cut off key Indian rivers and water sources that emanate from Chinese territory, if it so wished. As with Kashmir vis-à-vis Pakistan, New Delhi deploys diplomacy by senior MEA and government officials and agreement/treaties to try to resolve this territorial contestation, such as the 2005 Agreement on Political Parameters and Guiding Principles with China, which thus acts as a key national security tool. Increased trade connections and mutual interdependence is another means by which such threats can be potentially assuaged, although they only serve to finesse rather than entirely solve any problem. It is hoped that such positive interaction can overcome negative perceptions between the parties.

When we examine the territorial threat posed by Islamabad, the collective presence of multiple border contestations from both Pakistan and China heightens the sense of India's physical nature being endangered. Continued close China–Pakistan relations (including transfers of arms and nuclear technology) furthermore heighten Indian fears of encirclement. This presence is seen to threaten her wider national security interests, especially in terms of regional pre-eminence and her engrained desire to become a great power. China's building of ports in Pakistan, Myanmar, and Sri Lanka only bolsters this perception, which broadens to then include competition in the Indian Ocean via mutual naval expansion and mounting energy security competition. Alongside its exports to Pakistan, Beijing is also currently a major arms supplier to Bangladesh and Myanmar.

These core national security concerns relating to separatism, border security, and territorial extent, also apply to a number of India's smaller neighbours across South Asia. Hence, New Delhi is keen to help these countries to resist supporting/harbouring any groups that threaten India—be it either the separatists in the North-East, the Naxalites, or the terrorist groups trying to gain safe havens in India. In recent decades, India has worked with Nepal, Bhutan, and Bangladesh to remove militant bases from their territories as well as to improve the policing of borders versus destabilizing threats relating to the smuggling of drugs, fake currency, weapons, explosives, and people into India. New Delhi's influence via key treaty agreements with these countries help to achieve such aims.

Diplomatic negotiations again play into these dynamics and as a key means to ameliorate national security threats. In this regard, a joint census was carried out on disputed border areas with Bangladesh in July 2011, which resulted in a series of land swaps in 2015. Such efforts alleviated longstanding fears in New Delhi concerning the infiltration of Islamic and separatist militants into India, along with the negative influence of illegal immigration, and which further sought to lessen the occurrence of military confrontation between the two sides (as occurred in the 1990s). Deeper trade ties as well as energy cooperation have further amalgamated these approaches—in particular India's access to Bangladeshi gas and to Nepalese and Bhutanese hydroelectric power. In these ways, positive interaction can relieve negative perceptions concerning national security.

Further emblematic of these national security interests, and the fears inherent to them, India's relations with Myanmar has displayed a similar range of interaction. Thus, a series of memorandums of understanding (MoUs) have been put in place in the last two decades concerning stabilizing India's North-East and accessing Myanmar's hydroelectric power and gas reserves (the world's tenth highest). In this latter way, New Delhi has thus used its economic prowess to help achieve a national security aim by extending lines of credit to Myanmar's government, and funding gas and oil exploration projects, including the construction of pipelines.

Relating to border security, the resumption of high-level military-to-military interactions between India and Myanmar in 2000 has led to several joint military operations in their shared border areas. Aimed at tackling cross-border terrorism, Naypyidaw has dismantled several insurgent camps, while in June 2015 India was permitted to send troops into Myanmar's territory to attack rebel factions in an effort to reassert its regional control. Other joint ventures have included training Myanmar officials in anti-narcotics and anti-arms smuggling techniques, so as to better enhance Indian border security, as well as increasing trade, investment, and cultural ties to augment their cooperation and stability.

Societal Issues

National security in the internal sphere goes beyond the need to resolutely combat the plethora of separatist, insurgent, terrorist, and land dispute threats faced by India's leaders. Reiterating Maslow's hierarchy of needs, security not only relates to the physical domain in terms of law and order, stability, and freedom from fear but it also relates to meeting basic needs concerning access to food, water, warmth, and shelter. It also includes achieving the security of people physically as well as ensuring the essential protection of their employment, resources, family, health, and property.

In the present era, it is the pursuit of economic growth that is regarded as the best means by which all these forms of security can be achieved on the national level. Hence, from the early 1990s, there has been a political consensus in India to (slowly) embrace policies that promote economic liberalization and global engagement. Economic strength has emerged as the way to achieve domestic development and global great power status, while providing the financial means with which to embolden the tools integral to national security. These include modernizing her military or policing capacities to protect India's borders, trade routes, and overseas interests. India's vast population further acts as a vast consumer market that draws other countries to her.

The 2005 Manmohan (Singh) Doctrine summed up these perspectives, declaring that India's continued economic growth would concurrently bolster her internal modernization and prosperity, help stabilize the restive North-East, and heighten her international engagement and status. Safeguarding her energy security needs was also a key part of this equation (see Chapter 3). Such an aim was so vital that Manmohan Singh stated in 2012, '[I]f we do not increase the pace of the country's economic growth ... it most certainly affects our national security', indicating that economic advancement and progress were now associated with domestic stability. As per constructivism, it reveals the perception that such measures would reduce national threats.

As the extent of India's economic interaction has increased, there has also been an upsurge in the issues relevant to her national security, whereby alleviating poverty, enhancing development, and maintaining stability are now central and intertwined narratives for New Delhi. From this basis, there is considerable pressure on India to consistently attain high rates of economic growth. As such, the Planning Commission's Integrated Energy Policy of 2006 stated that an economic growth rate of 8 to 10 per cent was needed in the next 25 years to meet all of these developmental aims. Pursuing economic growth has thus become a dominant trait within her national security identity.

However, being an economy is transition from an inward-looking, socialist, and autarkic entity to something more globalized, liberalized, and confident, it has inculcated an array of anxieties, strains, and fears, putting pressure on the guiding principles of Indian society and its cultural basis. Especially in an age hall-marked by the greater interconnection and movement of people, ideas, products, and cultures, for a developing country such as India, there is an increase in disso-nance as inequalities widen, corruption opportunities increase, and environmental degradation proliferates. The demand for continued high rates of economic growth as part of the political consensus and culture within India's national identity will only serve to com-pound these issues.

While the policies of economic liberalization have led to an increase in India's middle class and a decline in relative poverty, it is estimated that between 200 and 300 million people still live in absolute poverty. Furthermore, over half of the Indian population does not have access to toilets or consistent water supply, while a third of people do not have access to elec-tricity. In turn, in 2013, the World Bank recorded that over 40 per cent of India's children are malnourished, the world's highest quantity. With a rapidly grow-ing population, such problems are also mounting in scope.

India's population is not only expanding quickly but it is also much younger than other major powers, with a median of 26.7 years versus 36.3 and 37.2, respectively, in China and the US. Although India currently experiences lower life expectancy and higher rates of child mortality, it is projected that by 2025 a fifth of the global population aged between 20 and 49 will be from India. Such figures will potentially give India the world's largest workforce and, if current growth persists, the world's largest economy by the middle of the twenty-first century.

There are positives concerning higher rates of economic output, such as more available funding for the domestic modernization aims of her leaders, as well as the enhancement of major national security tools such as her armed forces. However, such a large population could also perhaps act as an Achilles heel that drains significant resources away from government budgets. As such, New Delhi will need to fund massive future employment and social services programmes in a country where healthcare, housing, pensions, and education are all currently majorly underfunded.

As part of the dream of development, such funding will be a prerequisite for raising living standards and reducing the incidence of poverty, which are regarded as both the fait accompli of the Indian government's economic liberalization and as a way to enhance national security. Such provision will also go some way to lessen increasing social inequality and cultural dislocation, which can conceivably be translated into protest and unrest. With the urban population expected to rise to 590 million (or 40 per cent of the overall population) by 2030, such stresses would aggravate and would require long-term commitments for consistent infrastructure investment by ruling elites.

Generating intensifying social and economic tensions, as well as pressure on the government to maintain current levels of economic growth, these issues thus fall within the purview of national security. As such, they relate to not just the survival of India's population but also to the legitimacy of its ruling elites (and their core political ideals and aims), and they act as potential founts for instability within the Indian society. India's fast economic expansion has similarly proven hard to control, producing, for example, large fluctuations in inflation (at times exceeding 11 per cent), which puts pressure on many people, especially concerning the price of food.

For these reasons, with the help of the 2013 National Food Security Act, the Indian government introduced a US$21 billion enlargement of its national food subsidy programme to help mitigate these burdens. Although there was a political angle to such actions, these efforts complemented previous endeavours relating to subsidizing the price of petrol and diesel (which ended in 2015), all of which are designed to provide India's population access to food and warmth. The National Rural Employment Guarantee Act of 2005 similarly sought to relieve poverty by guaranteeing 100 days of unskilled employment to rural Indian households, in a bid to increase wages nationally, improve prosperity, empower women, and equalize pay levels across genders.

While we can certainly acknowledge the positive strides that the Indian government has made so far in improving the overall welfare of its population, at its heart inequality is increasing. Thus, although absolute poverty levels are in decline and life expectancy increased from 53.9 to 68.0 years between 1980 and 2014; in 2011, 21.3 per cent of Indians still lived on less than $1.90 a day. Although this figure stood at 50.3 per cent in 1987, it serves to contradict somewhat the aim of India's elites to lead a country of world-leading standing. In addition, immense social inequalities compound these viewpoints, with the richest 1 per cent in India owning 49 per cent of the national wealth in 2014—differences more severely exacerbated when urban areas are compared with poorer, rural ones.

Arguments further abound of a democratic deficit, whereby the key human rights of India's people concerning the provision of public goods such as education, health, and law and order, are not guaranteed. As such, in 2009, the number of non-government organizations in India exceeded the amount of primary schools and health centres provided by the state. Exceptionally low annual rates of tax collection (typically from 1 to 3 per cent of the population) and high rates of illegal capital flight only aggravate such issues. Ever-increasing levels of violent protests and strikes highlight rising discontent, with Chibba arguing that 'a rebellion by the poor and disenfranchised is conceivable in the absence of broad-based and sustainable social and economic progress' (Chibba 2011).

Underscoring how the delivery of public services falls within the remit of national security, and which is a major (and expanding) challenge faced by the Indian government, the issue of human rights is also a regular feature of her domestic landscape. Adhering to a mainly utilitarian outlook that privileges collective over individual rights, Indian society furthermore remains skewed towards patriarchal and male chauvinistic tendencies. Thus, while the Protection of Human Rights Act was passed in 1993, the death penalty remains in place, occurrences of torture by police and security forces remain rife, and poor working conditions are the norm (such as the regulation but not the banning of child labour). The smuggling, sale, and forced marriage of children also persevere, as do very high levels of female foeticide that are dramatically distorting gender ratios.

Such instances are acts of structural violence towards the population, which, because the Indian government is not adequately counteracting them, further represents the potential to become national security threats. As such, they are elements that place the safety of the population in a precarious position but also may be the catalyst for widespread political turbulence and violence. Certain features of Indian society facilitate such a situation, especially its highly rigid and hierarchical nature as shown via the caste system (despite the aims set out in the Constitution, see Chapter 1). India's frequently nepotistic political system, often based upon longstanding political inheritances and semi-feudal dynasties (as best personified by the Nehru–Gandhis, among many others), also highlights the deep-seated and personalized basis of inequality within Indian society.

Such a system inculcates possibilities for corruption, which have become more magnified in scale by India's recent acceptance of rapid economic liberalism and the ever-greater financial fruits that accompany it. Although it was present before liberalization, the post-1990s era of high growth and typically weak regulatory practices encourages corruption on an ever-increasing level and latitude. Widespread political and societal patronage—mainly through personal and social obligations to patrons, clients, and fellow caste

74

members—heightens such a problem. In recent years, major corruption scandals have involved politicians mis-selling national mobile licenses in 2011 by a staggering $38 billion, and have related to coal mining, water access, aviation, arms purchases, and the 2010 Commonwealth Games (which cost 15 times the original budget).

Apart from potentially leading to less foreign direct investment (FDI), and thus less economic growth, such incidences serve to delegitimize the authority of those in positions of power, and raise the spectre of protest, volatility, and major social unrest, especially when magnified by social inequities. In these ways, corruption is a national security threat to the stability of Indian society if it were ever to gain sufficient intensity or geographical scale. Furthermore, it also siphons (often public) money away from the ruling government, which could otherwise be used to enhance or fulfil the core domain and interest of development and great power. Overall, in 2014, India was ranked 85th on Transparency International's *Corruption Perceptions Index*, and this exemplifies how a national security threat can also endanger a country's international image by creating negative perceptions.

Another side effect of economic liberalization has been briskly increasing levels of environmental pollution, typically as a result of unchecked and badly regulated economic growth. In 2011, India was ranked as the fourth largest carbon emitter in the world with emissions of 566 million metric tons. Such emissions are deteriorating domestic air, land, water, and health quality, and the world's most polluted cities are now regularly located in India. Via escalating protest, unrest, and instability, domestic environmental destruction has the potential to delegitimize India's leaders. The Union Carbide gas leak in Bhopal in 1984, which led to over 15,000 deaths and 500,000 injuries, serves as a powerful historical example of the consequences of environmental pollution. More contemporarily, pollution levels were estimated in 2017 to lead to over one million premature deaths per year in India, along with reducing annual GDP levels by a significant 3 per cent.

Pollution is, therefore, another major threat to national security. On a fundamental level, it is an existential danger to the physical survival of India and, by extension, it can show the government's inability to suitably act as the guarantor of the safety, health, and well-being of its population—as per the remit of sovereignty that signifies the granting of authority for security from the people to elites. Resultant public health crises, especially concerning respiratory illnesses and childhood diseases, and the damaging of indigenous natural resources, are also all factors that represent a monumental present and future cost/threat that will hinder modernization and development. As with corruption, the issue is paradoxical in that the financial gains to be made from high economic growth have led to some unwanted, negative, and threatening societal consequences.

A Heady Mix

Within the internal sphere, India's leaders face a wide range of gestating issues and problems that can be considered as threats to the national security of their country. Some of these affect the territorial integrity of India, with 11 per cent of her territory under dispute from neighbouring entities, along with a host of related issues concerning insurgency, separatism, and terrorism. Beyond these more traditional aspects, we have observed a series of threats concerning the essential well-being and survival of her population—issues that are being amplified by New Delhi's policy of economic liberalization as the means to achieve modernization, development, and enhanced global status. Of these, corruption and pollution are the most existential and prominent dangers. Such threats endanger core aspects of India's national security identity, interests, and culture.

We can also see that the Indian government has a plethora of potent institutions and legislation designed to protect, encourage, and enhance national security. These represent a range of tools through which specific threats can be countered either by enacting particular legal provisions or via the deployment of security personnel and associated agencies. In this regard, Indian rulers can rein in regional states under centralized control and have the potential ability to apply severe and draconian emergency provisions (which have already been used on several occasions). They also possess a powerful range of security and intelligence services with which to monitor, regulate, and prosecute any part of the population that is deemed, in any way, to threaten national security.

In these ways, we can again witness how national security is a multifaceted entity whose myriad characteristics interact and interconnect with each other. Such an observation is evident in terms of the threats towards which it is directed (here, largely any group, body, or country acting against India's self-declared sovereignty and territorial basis). It is also visible how these threats interweave and interplay with our other core domains (most ostensibly concerning India's broader global and regional status but also her national values), and how the fruits of economic modernization and development can also be used to massage and enhance her bilateral relations. Fulfilling such interests depends on protecting India's national identity from such threats, and hence, as per our constructivist approach, their effective interaction in dealing with them.

What is furthermore recognizable is that many national security threats are mutually constructed and mutually constituted and rest upon historical interactions and inter-perceptions between actors. This is again a key facet of our constructivist basis concerning how threats are made. On a more intrinsic level, India has faced and continues to face a range of groupings whose aims are inimical to her own, be they separatists who wish to carve off a piece of Indian territory (thus attacking India's territorial integrity), or terrorists/insurgents who wish to pursue a different form of political organization (hence debilitating India's political system). At the root of these confrontations, including land disputes with other countries, is that the aims and interests of these actors—unless they are resolved—are opposed, irreconcilable, and mutually reinforcing. Victory for one side means defeat for the other, and any loss for one means a gain for the other.

From this basis, just as history, identity, culture, perception, and interaction are all critical factors in the delineation of India's national security, they are additionally of utmost importance to the national security of other states (and below that level, any other kind of domestic or international actor). Such a reflection is pertinent to the internal aspects of India's national security but is also highly evident in its external dimension, particularly in terms of competition between states but also between states and a variety of non-state actors, as will be demonstrated in Chapter 3.

3

The External Dimension

We now contemplate the external perspective of India's national security and delineate how—in an increasingly interconnected and globalized world—the successful attainment of domestic security is reliant upon a stable international environment. Such a basis furthermore reflects the dictum that a country's foreign policy is necessarily an extension of its domestic politics. Our analysis crucially incorporates many of the key institutions actively present in India, primarily the external focus/remit of core entities such as the PMO, the NSC, and the MEA, among others. As such, we first look at the role of India's armed forces and their capabilities, particularly in terms of preventing invasion and attack (including from their immediate neighbours) and also as a means to project Indian power and protect her interests within the regional and global spheres.

We then discuss how India's diplomatic and institutional capacities are deployed by her elites in order to prevent, isolate, and remove any threats to her, including New Delhi's political activity within multinational organizations vis-à-vis financial and environmental concerns. Common elements flourish between the domestic and international sides of New Delhi's national security equation, most typically the key importance given to attaining economic power. In these ways, we also debate economic, commercial, and energy security, and how these interact with India's military and diplomatic attributes. These requirements reflect the three domains deemed essential to our study of India's national security—chiefly modernization and great power, and its innate link to the defence of her sovereignty and territory and her democratic and secular values.

Finally, the necessity of India's diplomatic interactions, especially within a multilateral setting, remains pertinent as does her use of soft power capabilities. This discussion reminds us that national security is concerned with a plethora of different attributes beyond simply countries, and also echoes how the scope, scale, and character of national security threats (for India and indeed other countries) is continually fluctuating and shifting. The ongoing vital reference points of history, identity, culture, perception, and interaction will further continue to structure our examination. The use of Maslow's hierarchy of needs also remains relevant; especially concerning esteem needs relating to independence, status, dominance, prestige, and gaining respect from others. On the meta level, there is a similar need for self-actualization in terms of realizing potential and self-fulfilment—an aspect that directly relates to New Delhi's ingrained great power ambitions.

Armed Forces

Military power acts as one of the more immediate manifestations of national security, whereby a country's armed security forces can be deployed as a material means to actively, visibly, and tangibly counter a range of threats. In conjunction with domestic security forces in the guise of police and paramilitaries (see Chapter 2), armed forces are typically bolstered by their monopoly of violence within the context of the public law of a specific country. It is protecting this legitimate use of physical force that is the central aim of an army, air force, and navy, which frequently means effectively utilizing it against others so as to nullify their own use of coercive and hostile means.

In particular, military force is key to the conquering and control of territory and the protection of sovereignty—itself a core national security domain for India—and hence has both offensive and defensive expressions. The use of armies is the most apparent tactic within such contentions, while air power significantly expands the remit of such capabilities by being unencumbered by geographical boundaries, and hence enables a global reach. Much the same is true of naval power, whereby dominating the sea is additionally critical to securing trade routes. In these ways, military forces crucially interconnect the national and international environments, and are thus integral to the internal and external aspects or interests of India's national security.

Although largely detached from the realm of policymaking, attitudes towards the military and the use of force have morphed and evolved throughout the history of modern India. Hence, for Nehru such force was regarded as being of paramount importance for internal security and maintaining India's territorial sovereignty (and the initial period of consolidation in the 1940s and 1950s). It was, however, seen as irrelevant in the international sphere, at least until India's 1962 humiliation at the hands of China, which led to measures to suitably cultivate India's military capabilities. From then onwards, various leaders have initiated periodic modernization drives in order to boost India's self-sufficiency, self-reliance, and (for the BJP) global standing.

Such internal evolutions took place within the context of the expansion of New Delhi's security interests, which by extension has meant a consequent increase in national security threats. Thus, her military apparatus now encompasses remits ranging from traditional areas such as trade and energy security, to more emergent non-traditional capacities concerning transnational threats such as terrorism, piracy, smuggling, migration, and the environment. The adjustment from the early 1990s—of possessing an economy that was highly inward-looking to one that is actively interweaved with global liberal capitalism—further emboldened this enlarged range of interaction. It furthermore reflected a cultural shift concerning the role of the economy and its importance.

Apart from enhancing India's national autonomy, international status, and overall recognition, New Delhi's broadening power projection capabilities have encouraged a revolution in military affairs (RMA). The outward-looking economic policies of the last two decades have fuelled this focus. Resting upon the enhancement of reconnaissance, precision-strike, and command and control capabilities, India's spending on defence since 1997 has increased at an average annual rate of 6.3 per cent, and rose by 11 per cent for 2015–16 under Narendra Modi's BJP government. India's overall military budget rose from \$18.2 billion in 1988 to stand at $27.6 billion in 2000, before reaching $51.3 billion in 2015. In turn, expenditure as a percentage of GDP deteriorated from 3.7 per cent to 3.1 per cent to 2.3 per cent over the same period, and as a percentage of government spending accounted for 16.1 per cent, 12.0 per cent, and 8.7 per cent, respectively from 1988 to 2000 to 2015. Such percentage declines were more than offset by concurrent and rapid GDP growth rates (as detailed subsequently).

It is notable, however, that each of India's armed services has substantial capability shortfalls. Although modernization is regarded as the main means to overcome such issues, especially from a fiscal perspective concerning increased military budgets and more overall spending, India's democratic basis is also frequently seen as an obstacle in this regard. In combination with the military's subordinate role in the national security process, India's civilian policymakers have been historically resistant to empowering the military through the building of integrative procurement and joint-service structures, which could enhance the development and commissioning of new technologies. Such a perception (and resultant cultural trait) within India's broader national security identity thus serves to militate against a more effective modernization of her capabilities.

As per current modernization efforts across all of her armed services, India is presently positioned as the world's second-largest arms importer, and spent a total of $3.78 billion in 2015, which accounted for 13.2 per cent of the global total. Furthermore, for the period from 1990 to 2015, New Delhi had the world's highest overall arms imports—totalling $54.7 billion or 8.5 per cent of all such sales. A series of agreed purchases means that India will keep her pre-eminence in this area for several years to come, and she has various deals numbering over $100 billion to buy fighter jets, helicopters, landing ships, and submarines, which will all enrich her national security prowess. New Delhi's indigenous weapons production remains very low, totalling only $33 million in 2015, and it is unable to fully act as a national security resource to influence the imports of other nations.

Together, India's armed forces consist of the army, navy, air force, and coastguard, and these are under the management of the Ministry of Defence. Each service has their own chief of staff, while the de facto control of all branches rests with the prime minister of India (despite the fact that formal control rests with the Indian president, who is the supreme commander of the Indian Armed Forces). They are each organized into various tactical commands; totaling seven for the army (eastern, Kolkata; central, Lucknow; northern, Udhampur; southern, Pune; south-western, Jaipur; and western, Chandimandir), five for the air force (central, Allahabad; eastern, Shillong; southern, Thiruvananthapuram; south-western, Gandhinagar; and western, New Delhi), and three for the navy (western, Mumbai; eastern, Visakhapatnam; and southern, Kochi). Such positioning means that these tools are accessible across India, if and when required by her elites.

New Delhi carried out its first comprehensive review of national security in 1999, so as to improve the organization of India's military forces. The wide-ranging appraisal eventually led to the foundation of two joint commands to coordinate her three armed forces—the Strategic Forces Command (SFC) and the Far Eastern Naval Command (also known as the Andaman and Nicobar Command) established in the early 2000s. These can be headed by any of the armed forces. Furthermore, the review led to the introduction of a Nuclear Command Authority in charge of the country's nuclear weapons. India opened an overseas military air base in Farkhor in Tajikistan in 2007, and has set up naval staging and listening stations in Madagascar, Mauritius, and Seychelles. These developments have helped India project power beyond her borders and, in conjunction with her large armed forces, they can be regarded as a way of enhancing her security.

Capabilities

The Indian Army

As the primary tool within India's armed security forces, the Indian Army currently has somewhere close to 1.2 million active personnel, along with around 2.1 million reserve forces. As per this calculation, it is the world's third largest army behind China and North Korea. In addition, it has a high level of experience in terms of direct combat against other national militaries (primarily against Pakistan but also back in 1962 against China), in peacekeeping operations (across the smaller South Asian countries but also via United Nations Peacekeeping Operations, to which India has habitually been the world's third largest contributor), and in anti-insurgency and anti-terrorism activities (domestically within India, primarily in the North-East). Such attributes place the Indian Army at an advantage compared with most other forces in Asia. This has also led to the perception that the Indian Army is of utmost importance to India's national security.

As a result of such an experience, from which other countries wish to learn in order to counter their own particular national security issues, the Indian Army carries out an ever-growing number of exercises with the militaries of other states, thus augmenting India's interoperability capabilities. Such exercises have, for example, been conducted with regional countries like Bangladesh, Indonesia, the Maldives, and Singapore, as well as with many major world powers like the US, the UK, Russia, and China. Such exercises increase the prowess, skills, and knowledge of the Indian Army, and enhance its potential capabilities as an effective and a key national security tool. These interactions also facilitate positive ties with other countries by developing common threat perceptions.

Beyond using these capabilities to more ably protect India's sovereignty and territory, as well as more efficiently combat the myriad threats posed within its national security domain, New Delhi has leveraged its diplomatic strengths to establish a series of explicit defence agreements with countries in South East Asia (including Vietnam, Malaysia, Singapore, and Indonesia) and beyond (such as Australia, Brazil, and the US). By improving her linkages with other militaries, these pacts enhance interdependence and synergy with these countries, promoting stable relations that then aid India's pursuit and protection of her trade, energy, and political interests (discussed ahead).

As a further characteristic of this expertise, and also showing its potential to build stronger country-

to-country ties in the hope of enabling a safer and
more secure global environment (with a hoped for and
commensurate improvement of her national security),
India is also training personnel from other militaries. This endeavour includes the Afghan, Bahranian,
Qatarian, and Singaporean militaries, as well as the
Malaysian air force. More recently, the Indian Army has
taken on a non-traditional role within India, primarily
through domestic disaster relief, such as the ones after
the December 2004 tsunami in South India and the
September 2011 earthquake in Sikkim, and also following periodic bouts of flooding that affect large parts
of the country. These efforts help the Indian government to act against events that inculcate instability for
its people.

The Indian Air Force

With around 170,000 personnel, the Indian Air Force
(IAF) is highly experienced in terms of direct combat and operational experience. The IAF's historical
proficiency and combat interactions through India's
numerous conflicts have built this success. It also holds
annual exercises with many countries such as the US
and France, and is regarded as among the world's best.
Similar to the Indian Army, New Delhi is keen to

modernize the capabilities of the Indian Air Force, so as to gain parity with other countries in the world and to develop the most effective capacity it can to counteract any invasion or attack across India's extensive land and sea borders. The wide-ranging modernization is furthermore designed to increase its geographical reach, so as to project India's military power and protect its growing global interests. In this way, the IAF plays an integral task within India's national security interests and identity.

Organizationally, the IAF includes the Indian Space Research Organization (ISRO), which set up an aerospace command in 2007 and has the renowned capacity to launch communications and earth observation satellites into geosynchronous orbit as well as lunar probes. In this regard, India has established itself as a leading commercial provider of such skills and has put satellites into orbit on behalf of many countries from her Sriharikota launch centre in Andhra Pradesh. India is also considered to have the world's second highest number of remote-sensing satellites, a capability which it deploys to monitor its myriad internal threats (especially from the Naxalites), and which serves to heighten her intelligence collection capabilities against such vulnerabilities. In February 2017, ISRO launched 104 satellites in one rocket, the most attempted in history.

The Indian Navy

Currently totalling somewhere in the region of 55,000 active personnel, the Indian Navy has successfully deployed to all the major bodies of water in the world. Its strategic remit includes guaranteeing the security of the Indian Ocean Region (IOR), which is vital to the defence of India's maritime borders, as well as safeguarding her trade and security interests in the region. Primarily, these are to secure the transportation of gas and oil from West Asia, including keeping the Straits of Hormuz open to ensure an uninterrupted energy supply (known as the 'Hormuz Dilemma') and to preserve sea lines of communication (SLOCs) that are essential to her rising export and import of goods, commodities, and products to and from across the world.

More broadly, India's current maritime build-up and modernization is further directed at preserving regional stability, strengthening New Delhi's peacekeeping capacity, and ensuring the ongoing domination of the IOR as her natural domain. To bolster these interests, India had two aircraft carriers in service by 2016 (INS Viraat and INS Vikrant) and has plans to build several others in the next decade, a capability that would place her second only to the US. The Indian Navy conducts regular large-scale exercises with several global and regional actors including the US, France, China, Australia, Japan, Nigeria, Mozambique, and South Korea, as well throughout South East Asia with Brunei Darussalam, Indonesia, and Singapore, among others. Key to her energy and trade security, and her modernization and great powers goals, the Indian Navy is intrinsic to the realization of these interests as a part of India's national security identity.

Nuclear Forces

As the ultimate exemplar of destructive force projection within the international sphere, India also possesses nuclear weapons. Stemming from decades of research that mirrored her efforts to develop nuclear power plants (which included the Peaceful Nuclear Explosion of 1974), the BJP-led Indian government eventually tested nuclear weapons in May 1998. Based on a no-first-use posture, whereby India will only use its weapons after a nuclear attack, it is estimated that New Delhi has an arsenal of about 110 warheads and enjoys a nuclear triad (the ability to launch weapons from land, air, and sea) to a maximum range of 5,500 kilometres. Such a capacity can be seen to enhance her national security in terms of dissuading enemies from attacking her, but it is also basically unusable in combatting small non-state actors such as terrorists, or against low-level attacks (such as Pakistan's at Kargil in 1999), and is thus principally symbolic.

Economic Security

Within the present era, economic growth can be seen as the fundamental aim of the Indian government and that of virtually all of her political parties (except the Communist entities). Immediately critical to modernizing India and transitioning the country from being developing to developed, along with raising New Delhi's stature internationally to become a great power, an expanding economy (as we have already seen in Chapter 2) is now the *sine qua non* of her national security. It is, thus, a key pillar of India's identity as per its positive perception à la constructivism. Modernization aids and assuages any number of threats to the state and allows for the building up of appropriate resources to protect India's sovereignty and territorial integrity—primarily the armed forces noted above. Trade additionally creates interdependence with her neighbours and other countries through win-win agreements premised upon mutual growth.

The other virtue of economic growth in the national security sphere is its highly translatable and convertible nature. Evident across her range of domestic and international interactions, India's economic prowess can be transformed into political power through 'commercial diplomacy' that draws other states to India, and which can be further utilized as an influence in negotiations or transmuted into assurances of loans or aid. Globally, economic strength can give New Delhi enhanced standing in multilateral institutions, hence representing a form of 'institutional' or 'structural' power. In both cases, such a conversion can be used to further India's national security outlook by crafting the international environment towards her interests.

Therefore, as the core lynchpin of her contemporary political trajectory, and as the apparent answer to meeting her national security interests (and counteracting the threats inherent to them), India's pursuit of economic growth necessitates a global level of interaction. Such economic exchanges rest upon gaining India's industrial base the things it needs to produce goods for sale (principally raw materials and commodities), along with the means to fuel this production (primarily oil and gas) as well as providing the regional and global markets within which these outputs can be sold and profited from. Conversely, India's population offers a huge market that is attractive to other economies. In spite of these strengths, it has many unwanted side effects and consequences such as corruption, environmental damage, unrest, and inequality.

Fully appreciating the potential of these mutually beneficial connections typifies India's interaction in this sphere, along with the recollection and shock of the 1991 balance-of-payments crisis (during which the country came close to bankruptcy and had to request an emergency loan from the International Monetary Fund). From this basis, and with an average annual growth rate of 5.7 per cent and 6.9 per cent in the 1990s and 2000s respectively, India has slowly emerged as a leading and indispensable economic behemoth on the world stage. Her growth rate stood at 7.3 per cent in 2015. Such incremental growth is bolstering the perception that economic growth is central to security.

In 2015, India's economy was the fourth largest in the world (in price purchasing parity terms) with a GDP of \$8.06 trillion—behind the US on \$17.97 trillion, the European Union on \$19.18 trillion, and China on \$19.51 trillion. Proportionately, India further represented over 7.0 per cent of the global GDP. Most of this strength is based on IT, software, and services, which equalled 45.0 per cent of the economy in 2015, with 29.7 per cent being based in industry and 17.0 per cent in agriculture. Given that India is currently the world's 11th largest importer and the 20th largest exporter, there is still considerable room for expanding these capabilities globally. Therefore, as her economic clout rises so will its continued criticality vis-à-vis her national security interests.

It is also important to highlight the role played by the Indian diaspora, who are referred to as Persons of Indian Origin (PIOs) or Non-Resident Indians (NRIs). Making up the world's second largest such grouping (of over 25 million individuals), the diaspora are an important financial source for New Delhi, sending back remittances. Frequently world-leading, and amounting to 1–2 per cent of her annual GDP, such payments are critical to the Indian economy on a local or micro level. In turn, the diaspora provide a physical and cultural link between the motherland and the country they reside in, and act—in many instances—as the public face of India abroad. As per constructivism, history, culture, identity, and interaction all inform its importance. New Delhi has occasionally deployed its armed forces to aid parts of the diaspora, most notably the 1990 Kuwait airlift of 110,000 expatriates, and the 2011 exodus from Libya (via Indian warships).

We must, however, note that India's acceptance of liberal globalized economics has been slow, precisely because many of her leaders saw such a system as innately threatening. This sentiment stems in part from the negative experiences of colonialism and imperialism by external forces, especially by Great Britain, which siphoned off India's national wealth in order to boost its own standing in the world. As such, prior to the 1991 crisis, international finance was itself regarded as a national security threat against India's sovereign and independent basis and autonomy. It was also viewed as a hazard to India's way of life that was able to dilute her indigenous cultures. In these ways, history's influence continues to impact elite perceptions of the international system and, by extension, inform her present interactions within it as per her broader identity.

Such caution and suspicion, courtesy her negative colonial experiences, underscores the continued role of history, memory, and experience in New Delhi's global interactions, and still permeates the making of India's economic policy to this day. It also highlights the evolving, shifting, and permeable nature of national security in that the factors that are considered threats at one time can be transformed to become positives at another. Much of the same is true of India's allies, with the US being regarded with mistrust during the Cold War, but now seen as a key partner. Across all these levels, historical memory thus persists as a vital touchstone of national security and also shows us how history and its recollection is not necessarily either static or permanent.

New Delhi's approach towards globalization remains balanced between seeing the rewards of global engagement (via the associated trade, FDI, technology, and market benefits that it brings) and state protection (versus multinationals that assault local businesses, and foreign ideas that pressure native philosophies). The 1997 Asian Financial Crisis underscored such viewpoints, when (western) external investment was removed from states across South East Asia that had hastily liberalized their economies, causing the devastation of their financial structures. International law, 'western' ideas, and stock market/commodity speculation are hence all seen as undesirable and putatively undermining extra-national pressures.

These ideas buoy nationalists within India who frequently present the country as being under duress from external forces that seek to undermine her global standing. This contention has been particularly true of the BJP who, in the 1980s and 1990s, explicitly campaigned against the presence of foreign corporation in India (such as their anti-Kentucky Fried Chicken agitations, and their 1996 election slogan of 'Computer chips, not potato chips'). Although the party can now be argued to fully desire capitalism in its global form, such nationalist tensions fuel popular pressure on ruling elites to be more strident on the international stage and concerning specific issues (such as land disputes). They must thus be factored into India's national security equation.

Ultimately, those governing from New Delhi must balance these elements to act in the country's national (security) interests, and it is the role of India's diplomats within the MEA to be the critical human interface between governmental policy and their realization in the global domain. The MEA's key functions are data collection, policy formulation, and policy implementation, through a focus on specific bilateral relations and multilateral institutions. It also houses the Public Diplomacy Division, created in 2006, which engages the Indian public in international affairs. While the MEA is regarded as a key national security tool, it is currently understaffed in comparison with many other countries, and has only 900 active personnel—half the number of China's and less than a twentieth of the US's—which may result in less diplomatic skill/success.

Apart from New Delhi's commercial diplomacy that negotiates and establishes new trading relationships and agreements with other countries for the overall national benefit, it is the ability to secure energy sources that is of paramount concern in her external relations. Without these supplies, many areas of industrial production would potentially stall, as India's own domestic resources are lacking in hydrocarbons in the form of oil and gas. While the country is strong in terms of coal reserves (mining 6.2 per cent of the world's total annual output, while consuming 7.5 per cent—the world's third highest usage), and has supplies said to last 200 years, this capacity is unfortunately a highly polluting and unsustainable energy resource. India does, however, have an established capacity to harness nuclear energy, and the nascent capability to produce solar and wind power, although these are currently not fully developed to meet the country's ever-burgeoning needs.

By extension, and on a more fundamental level, the production of energy across all of these areas is highly multipurpose when we are concerned with its importance for India's population. As per Maslow's hierarchy of needs, at its most basic, energy helps to provide warmth and the means to cultivate or produce food (as per biological and physiological needs), while access to resources and health are core safety needs, which collectively inculcate, preserve, and encourage social stability.

In addition, providing the appropriate fruits of modernization in terms of raising living standards and—under a neoliberal capitalism model—material/consumable goods, is also deemed vital. As India's emerging middle class (who are increasingly living in cities and urban environments) grows, the domestic demand and consumption of energy will also rise. Power will also be needed to run accompanying transport services and modern amenities that such segments of the population will demand as part of the India's wider national development. As such, and as per its definition by the United Nations as 'the continuous availability of energy in various forms and in sufficient quantities at reasonable prices', energy security remains critical to a wide range of key national security interests, issues, and constituents. As former External Affairs Minister Jaswant Singh has noted, '[E]nergy is security; ... any deficiency ... will compromise the nation's security' (Ogden 2014b: 63).

Further up Maslow's hierarchy, a constant and unremitting supply of energy is the key ingredient not only to continued economic growth and development but also for heightening India's great power status. The ability to project power in order to safeguard interests through the control of key geographical areas or globally important resources is also the hallmark of such power. In these ways, therefore, energy security again serves as an example that binds together many divergent yet crucially interconnected and inter-reliant parts of India's national security jigsaw. Its attainment affects agriculture, industry, services, households, and even government legitimacy and, as Manmohan Singh states, '[T]he quest for energy security is second only ... to food security' (Ogden 2017: 94). From this basis, energy security is a central pillar of India's identity, which is built upon the specific demands faced by her population as per the particular circumstances of the country.

Added to this centrality is the assertion that as India's economy continues to growth, so will her energy needs. In addition, the Indian population is also increasing in size, a factor of ever-greater importance given its younger profile in the context of longer life expectancy and falling infant mortality. In combination, South Asia's most important country will have world-leading attributes in both of these abovementioned areas in the coming decades, which, in turn, will require even more energy, whose usage is set to rise at least fivefold in the next 10–15 years, if not by more. Within these dynamics, she will become a major oil importer (the world's third largest) and by 2020 it is estimated that at least 90 per cent of her energy requirements will have to be found via external sources.

It is for these very important reasons that New Delhi has a non-discerning and non-discriminatory attitude concerning how her diplomats and corporations access oil and gas abroad. As such, India will quite happily engage with countries that have poor records vis-à-vis internal governance and human rights, despite her own self-avowed democratic credentials. New Delhi thus has a non-ideological and unconditional approach to purchasing energy resources, which often gives her an advantage versus western countries that are sometimes more wary in their methods. The perception among her leaders that energy security is vital therefore conditions these interactions.

India buys energy resources from countries frequently seen as pariahs in the international system, such as Iran, Sudan, Myanmar, and some Central Asian states, whereby any criticism is outweighed by New Delhi's more crucial energy and economic security concerns. The majority of India's crude oil imports come from West Asia (primarily via Saudi Arabia and Iraq), followed by Africa (half of which comes from Nigeria), Latin America (mainly from Venezuela), and some small amounts from South East Asia and Central Asia. The MEA is endeavouring to diversify India's supply—particularly away from the restive West Asian region—so as to offset any regional crises or geopolitical shocks that may unexpectedly reduce or even curtail her supply.

Overall, in 2015, the country was the world's fourth largest oil consumer, importing 4.1 million barrels per day (4 per cent of the global total), and indigenously made approximately 1 million barrels per day (just over 1 per cent of the global total). In 2005, New Delhi also set up a Strategic Petroleum Reserve so as to build up an emergency store in case of an external calamity or sudden price rise. Indian conglomerates, primarily the partially state-owned Essar, GAIL, ONGC, and Reliance Industries, lead the process of acquiring energy rights in other countries, frequently aided by the MEA, including access to India's sizeable foreign exchange reserves to boost competitiveness. On occasion, such links have reduced the autonomy of these multinationals, mainly concerning the MEA signing off on proposed bids and having smaller budgets than their larger competitors.

All of these endeavours rest upon the ability to control the IOR, the world's third largest body of water extending from Australasia to Africa. Such control is the best means to ensure that external supplies of oil and gas will reach India unhindered by any threat of piracy or attack, and explains, in part, the rapid expansion of her maritime armed forces to become the best of any IOR littoral country. In turn, it is estimated that 70 per cent of the world's petroleum products will transition the IOR (either to reach South Asia or the Asia-Pacific regions), while around 90 per cent of all Indian trade relies on sea transportation. For all of these reasons, it is a national security prerequisite for New Delhi to project Indian power downwards into the region—either physically via the Indian Navy or diplomatically via agreements with other regional actors.

Given the many pressures that India currently faces concerning her acquisition of energy supplies in the form of oil and gas in conjunction with their ever decreasing nature/incidence, New Delhi has sought to improve the production of energy from other sources. A leading contender has been nuclear energy and, by 2016, India had 21 active nuclear reactors with at least another 6 under construction, and long-term plans for them to produce 50 per cent of her energy needs by 2045. Arguably, producing cleaner energy—at least compared with coal-fired power stations—they have the potential to reduce pollution as well as to diminish an over-reliance upon oil and gas imports.

India's plentiful thorium reserves, used to fuel some of these plants, further act as a means to heighten her self-sufficiency. The MEA has also signed a number of agreements with uranium-rich countries (such as Australia, Mongolia, Canada, Kazakhstan, and Namibia) to additionally aid energy production over a protracted period of time. New Delhi has also been able to gain investment from several countries to build nuclear reactors—such as France, Japan, Russia, South Korea, and the US. To hedge against any associated risks, India further passed the Nuclear Liability Act in 2010 that holds foreign suppliers responsible for any accidents that take place at plants that they have erected in India for a period of 100 years after construction. Such legislation can be seen as an effective insurance against a perceived national security threat, whilst the debate concerning its implementation invoked strong historical fears of malign western intentions towards New Delhi.

In terms of other production, New Delhi is furthermore attempting to diversify its means of energy production, with the same aims of ensuring a steady supply along with enhancing autonomy and protecting against negative side effects such as pollution and associated protest. In these ways, the last decade or so has seen a concerted focus on establishing renewable and clean sources in the form of biomass, hydropower, wind, solar, and tidal energy. Signing agreements with neighbours who have advanced hydropower resources (such as Bangladesh, Nepal, and Sri Lanka) has emboldened these efforts. It is of note though that, just as with nuclear reactors, the upfront costs of such projects are high and the benefits will take time to be realized. In turn, promoting more efficient means of production will also deliver higher eventual rewards.

Diplomacy and Soft Power

It is not only through hard and coercive means such as its armed forces or mutual economic gains that a country can improve its national security environment. Indeed, the use of direct force is quite an uncommon feature in contemporary international affairs and even where it does occur, it can incur reputational damage, sanctions, and isolation for those who use it in an offensive capacity. Instead, it is diplomacy on a bilateral—country-to-country—or a multilateral level—with multiple countries simultaneously—that takes precedence, which for India is carried out through its diplomats and ambassadors in the MEA and through the statesmanship of its leaders in the NSC.

Further, moving beyond a material or financial form of interaction as presaged upon military or economic quotients, such exchanges rest upon ideational elements—that is the identity of countries and the values and culture that make them, as per constructivism. Thus, the very idea of a country—of India—is of importance. Here, national principles that complement the core domain of democracy and secularism help build a convivial image of India, which then bolster her country-to-country ties. These attitudes can thus build solid relationships based upon mutual interests and threats (thus underscoring how national security has an international perspective). Overall, they serve to help create and sustain a peaceful, stable, and protected environment that can fundamentally aid the general realization of her three core national security domains.

Such understandings also allow us to deepen our level of analysis by highlighting how security is country and context specific, producing a very focused, explicit and particular emphasis that will vary from country to country. It also confirms the highly existential nature of national security, whose function is to preserve a society versus (and at its most extreme, at the expense of) others. As part of international diplomacy, the very values that a country wishes to preserve can also conversely act as a tool of preservation, through a process that is reinforcing and self-referential. Our core emphasis on history, identity, culture, perception, and interaction form these notions.

Within a multilateral setting, it is finding commonality with the values, interests, and fears of others that is central to success. With different institutions having different foci—from those directly concerned with military and security matters to others engaged in economic discussions—such unity/harmony of approach concerning espoused national principles allow for successful agreement. Furthermore, these regimes function through certain rules and practices, themselves derived from shared world views, and by chronological extension, from common historical experiences. Such mechanisms have a reinforcing aspect by their formulation and repetition, and thus serve to bring their members closer by nurturing interdependence, mutuality, and stability.

In these ways, Indian leaders and diplomats have been, for example, able to build institutions such as the Non-Aligned Movement (NAM) based upon their anti-colonial, anti-imperialist, non-interference, and peaceful values, and a concern for the pro-developing world, whereby the other members were able to see a congruence of concerns with New Delhi. If such a basis had not existed, NAM wouldn't have existed either. It was thus specifically dependent upon India's identity and wider cultural traits. As would prove to be the case with other groupings, such a coalescence of viewpoints also adds legitimacy to them, and through her leadership of the NAM, New Delhi was able to gain acceptability and support for her favoured view of the world.

In the United Nations, India has also largely found a natural home through an international organization whose founding values echoed those of New Delhi concerning peace and security, cooperation, a belief in international law to settle disputes, and a commitment to development. India's democratic basis is also a major fillip within this grouping, along with her contributions to UN Peacekeeping Operations that confirm her fundamental belief to it. Being in the UN also allows India to help shape debates, outcomes, and responses to major matters of global importance, primarily international terrorism and climate change— both of which appear to be existential threats to India by endangering her political, territorial, and current modernization basis. It also validates, and thus protects, shared values concerning democracy and secular tolerance.

Underpinning all of these merits, India is striving to gain a permanent veto set on the UN Security Council, which, if achieved, would substantially strengthen her national security by making her inviolable to international criticism and sanctions. She would also be able to extend protection to others, giving her extra leverage in negotiations. The advantages that such a position would bring, and which acts as the contemporary holy grail of all diplomatic tools, would significantly aid her efforts to combat and eradicate the host of threats faced by her elites. As her global, especially economic, centrality rises, gaining such a status will become more likely.

Akin to her attitude towards globalization and the benefits of neoliberal economics, belonging to a multilateral grouping also requires some loss of sovereignty, particularly concerning agreeing to international treaties which are binding and control the actions/behaviour of their signatories. However, this balancing or trade-off bears much resemblance to other actors that we have already seen concerning India's national security whereby one gains (say economic growth) results in an unwanted side effect (pollution), but whose negative impact New Delhi then seeks to control. This (some may say, inevitable) paradox informs the central dilemma of the national security policy.

Notwithstanding this cost-benefit equation, as India's economic prowess continues to rise and she becomes ever more central to the calculations of others (as a trading destination and market), so too will New Delhi's overall standing in the international system. Along with such pre-eminence, India's voice in multilateral forums will become commensurately louder, giving her policymakers more influence among their peers. It will also give India the ability to shape the world in its own image, just as other major powers have done, and to build a global system that more readily promotes, confronts, and protects New Delhi's core interests, concerns, and fears. This influence will be acutely apparent concerning climate change, terrorism, trade, and finance. It will also allow India's leaders to transmit their national identity and culture on the global stage.

It is from this basis that the very image that India presents to the world becomes of significance to the contours, nature, and delivery of her national security. This assertion directly confirms the efficacy of our constructivist approach concerning identity. On the macro level, this argument's efficacy is clear—if New Delhi were to be more belligerent and aggressive in its external affairs, for example, offensively and systematically invading others, inciting war and conflict, and upsetting regional/global diplomatic balances, then its security and environment would deteriorate to the detriment of her national security. Conversely, if India's leaders sought to present their country as a benign, convivial, and positive partner, then this would lessen threats towards her, but it could also make the country vulnerable to opportunism and bullying by others, as per her history.

As we have seen, the attitude of New Delhi has firmly rested within the latter approach, but with a persistent undertone of suspicion, distrust, and frequently asserted autonomy and, in the current era, it is highly cognizant of the virtues of soft power. A very different kind of power, which complements the mélange of power types we have already encountered—institutional, legal, military, economic, and diplomatic—soft power is described by Joseph Nye as 'the ability to get what you want through attraction rather than coercion or payments ... (enacted via) a country's culture, political ideals, and policies' (Nye 2004). Strictly non-material, soft power rests upon elements of aspiration, identity, and commonality that serve to effectively allure actors together.

Mirroring the ability to build a consensus of opinion within a multilateral setting, the guiding essence of soft power is to bring other countries towards your world view. This emboldens the values and principles underpinning such a vision, hence legitimizing and normalizing it (globally). A form of international credibility and kudos, soft power is vital to our discussion of national security as it acts as a tool to shape perceptions and mindset of others towards India, and which can have commensurate benefits concerning her strategic, economic, and diplomatic quotients. That stated, having solid material (economic) capabilities can aid initial inter-country connections.

Via the prism of soft power, India—along with (on some level) all other countries in the international system—is seeking to project, promote, and protect a certain national brand. While less effective regionally, given the unsettled nature of relations with Pakistan and China, and her overwhelming dominance over smaller South Asia countries, New Delhi is keen to promote a certain kind of *Indian* soft power. Institutionally, the MEA's Public Diplomacy Division and the Indian Council for Cultural Relations are the major fulcrums through which soft power is enacted, primarily to present India as a diverse, pluralistic, and harmonious multicultural society. Reflecting key facets of her national identity as constructed by her historical interaction, soft power is a political diplomacy tool that is also embodied by the behaviour of her citizens abroad.

To this end, by 2016, the Indian Council for Cultural Relations had established 36 cultural centres in other countries with the aim of endorsing India via the strengthening of mutual national ties. Such cultural diplomacy includes the promotion of Indian dance, music, photography, theatre, and visual arts, as well as the translation of classical texts written in Sanskrit into other languages.

Typifying their adherence to key Indian values, in 1965, the Council instituted the Jawaharlal Nehru Award for International Understanding to reward individuals encouraging international understanding, goodwill, and friendship via Nehruvian values of peace, secularism, and tolerance.

Other examples abound of efforts to employ India's cultural capital as a way to raise her international recognition, so as to amalgamate a positive image of India abroad and ameliorate her wider national security environment. The Bollywood industry leads the way in this regard with its worldwide appeal, as do her cuisine, sporting activities success (principally cricket), and literature. These are all cultural exports that resonate particular values, build up the aura of India, and fundamentally act as a form of public relations aimed at widening her worldwide appeal by simultaneously instilling familiarity and credibility, and thus national legitimacy and favourability.

Creating such a climate and reputation enhances Indian power by making other countries more inclined to positively adhere to and follow her national values, thus fostering interaction, synergy, and interdependence. Such benefits can then be translated into better diplomatic ties in the more traditional (economic/ military) areas, which we have previously analysed, with further benefits then trickling down into related national security domains—in particular modernization and great power but also bolstering her democracy and secularism, and legitimizing her sovereign basis. Core political values of non-violence, democracy, and peaceful mediation are all imperative here, and serve to underscore the validity of our analytical approach resting upon constructed identity.

In more recent leaders, Prime Minister Narendra Modi has been explicit in his attempts to promote the country via a 'Brand India' campaign, which seeks to enrich India's global standing. An early success was the introduction (on 21 June 2015) of the first International Yoga Day that was achieved through heavy lobbying of the international community by Indian diplomats at the United Nations. Such an event is telling in that this festival innately celebrates and conjoins with key Indian national values relating to peace, harmony, non-coercion, and mediation, and is therefore a means with which to project India's national identity into the international system. On a highly micro level, such an observation confirms the interconnected nature of national security, whereby ideational/material factors coalesce and values notify real-world policymaking.

More profoundly, soft power and the links that it displays towards other kinds of power—and their ongoing applicability to the heady cocktail that is national security—reflects many of this book's key themes. As such, and as per our constructivist basis, identity, values, and culture are all key ingredients that are integral to deciphering soft power, as are history (the process by which these elements are founded and engrained) and interaction (as the means by which commonality and difference between countries are realized). Finally, within Maslow's hierarchy of needs, self-image is a crucial (initial) stage of the process towards achieving self-actualization. In our globalized and information-driven age, the attainment of such goals gains greater credence.

Inside/Outside

In the present era, India's national security pertains as much to the world outside her borders as it does to her internal dynamics. The guiding basis of her core security apparatus—here principally her armed forces in various guises, along with her diplomatic and soft power capabilities—typifies this duality, as does the functioning of her now firmly outward-oriented economy. Within an international environment ever more presaged upon increased interaction and globalization, such a focus has become a necessary part of her national security calculations, and one that is perennially expanding and escalating in its collective scope, scale, and importance.

This characteristic encompasses material sides of India's national security dynamics, such as the physicality and modernization of her army, air force, and navy, as well as her growing economic prowess. To this aspect are then intermingled its ideational aspects—most notably her national values, brand, and self-image. Again, these facets underscore the complexity of national security and its realization, along with how these elements (and other related aspects in the external and the internal domains) are interweaved, inter-reliant, and essentially international. What unifies them is their shared purpose to maximize India's national security via the three core domains of democracy and secularism, sovereignty and territory, and modernization and great power.

Such interconnection links New Delhi's national security interests, fears, and concerns from the internal to the external (and back) in several ways. Most profoundly, it reinforces the centrality of economic development and its attendant search for energy supplies, commodities, markets, and consumers. It also highlights how her security forces can be used to control and mediate both the domestic and international environments (including creating positive interdependence with other countries). Finally, it also shows how a core national identity informs the very being of India that not only structures her persona abroad but which is converted into a soft power repository that is designed to protect, embolden, and safeguard the wider global sphere, so as to heighten her national security.

It is from within this complexity that most features of India's domestic politics and international affairs can be argued to fall within the purview of national security. Partially, this holistic quality involves the very nature of the world and its interactional basis—through which few countries act in isolation and their primary forms of enhancement rest upon exchange. As we have also seen, this entanglement further conjoins the micro level to the macro, whereby, for example, the warmth needs of an individual citizen depend upon inter-country energy security diplomacy and any range of other elements in between (maritime security, border security, financial security, and so on). It thus verifies how the study of national security is relevant to all of us but also that it is a relative phenomenon that is specific to different situations.

Conclusion
A Continued Evolution

National security holds a relevance and importance that goes beyond mere internal stability. Its significance includes the well-being and prosperity of citizens and the populations they form, as well as the relations between all countries on a regional and global basis. At the fulcrum of domestic politics and governance and as the mainstay of international affairs, upholding national security is the raison d'être of any country's existence. Although 'national' in designation, at its heart and due to its interactional, relative, and inter-connected nature, security is inalienably *international*.

Due to its complexity, which is ever-growing in intricacy and density as more interests, threats, and fears enter its contemporary orbits, national security—

for India and for other actors—must be regarded as being continually evolving. New Delhi's own experiences since Independence point to such an attribute, as India's expanding global interaction and status have led to her increased level of global participation and a corresponding widening of national security issues. A more visible, resource-hungry, and trade-dependent India has necessitated this involvement, along with the greater and growing diversity of threats that she faces, internally as well as externally. This change has come both from within India itself and also from a shifting international system.

Here, we evaluate and reflect on the constructivist approach laid out in this book concerning our focus on core principles relating to history, identity, culture, values, and interaction, before appraising the appropriateness and applicability of Maslow's hierarchy of needs. We then consider how successful New Delhi's current performance is in effectively responding to, curtailing, and even nullifying the host of threats challenging India. All of this leads us to consider the central quandary facing the study of national security—in India and elsewhere—of paradox and parallax, and how complete freedom from threat for countries is essentially unobtainable, and that as a field of study it is in reality far more concerned with national *insecurity*.

Evaluation

We have described the major facets, actors, and tools that are inherent to national security, and how their analysis can help indicate what is specific to the Indian context. Deploying a constructivist approach premised upon the inclusion of identity-focused factors that go beyond more military (realist) and solely material-based accounts, our analysis unveiled the nature, delivery, and extent of Indian national security. To aid this analytical foundation, we also used Maslow's hierarchy of needs to show the range of requirements that national security must meet.

Analytical Attributes

- *History*: Highlighted the origins and roots of New Delhi's national security concerns from badly demarcated borders—legacy of the colonial occupation (and the consequent territorial conflicts across India's borders)—to engrained conflict and tension with Pakistan (through repeated conflict). India's wariness of the international system as a whole, as well as the desire of her leaders to enhance their country's position in it (and inherently to ensure its continued survival), also stems from such anti-imperial and anti-colonial urges.

- *Identity*: Revealed that there are specific and particular elements that characterize a uniquely Indian perspective concerning what is important vis-à-vis her national security behaviour. The distinctive nature of India's political system (and focus on democracy and secularism) as well as her physical outline (as per her desired borders in South Asia) and her guiding self-image (to become a modern great power in the twenty-first century) all derive from this basis. Just as India has its own viewpoint on national security, so too will others.

- *Culture*: Confirmed that context-specific histories, experiences, memories, and identities produce country-specific cultures. From this basis, India's past (and how it is recalled by her leaders and then juxtaposed with future national ambitions) denotes a precise form of exclusivity that advises how her policy is made and the preferences upon which it is based. The repetition of key ideas, fears, interests, conflicts, and agreements serve to formulate this culture, making it distinguishable from more short-lived sets of values and principles.

- *Perception*: Underscored that the various perspectives of its leaders, elites, and institutions influence the delineation of national security. By informing the formation of national identity and national culture, such perceptions aid our understanding of which interests are of most importance to national security and, by extension, which threats are then challenging these interests. Importantly, perceptions can change—especially concerning the meaning of history and its recollection or memory, which underlines their importance.

- *Interaction*: Acknowledged that national security tasks are not performed in isolation, and that a country's interests, desires, issues, and fears are all dependent upon exchanges with others—either in the past, the present, or the future. Equally, while we can analyse Indian national security, other countries have their own corresponding sets of national security interests, desires, issues, and fears specific to *their* history, identity, culture, and perception. Interaction, coalescence, and divergence across these zones regulate *international* security.

Maslow's Hierarchy

As per Figure C.1, Maslow's hierarchy of needs determined the different levels of needs that national security must meet, as per the granting of sovereignty by a population to her leaders. The host of security concerns raised in this book mapped onto each of the diagram's levels, with basic biological needs pertaining to the supply of water, food, warmth, and shelter being followed by larger (societal) safety needs concerning employment, access to resources, family, health, and property. All of these elements directly correlated with internal national security interests and aims.

Further up the scale, the esteem needs—of independence, status, dominance, prestige and respect from others—specifically related to sovereignty and territorial issues, along with India's long-sought quest

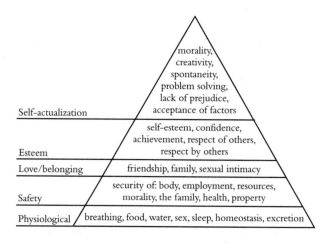

FIGURE C.1: Maslow's Hierarchy of Needs
Source: https://commons.wikimedia.org/wiki/
File:Maslow%27s_Hierarchy_of_Needs.svg, under distribution by Creative Commons Attribution, CC BY-SA 3.0.

to become a great power in the international system. At the zenith of the hierarchy are self-actualization needs regarding realizing potential and self-fulfilment. Of note is that our analysis did not include the middle level of love or belonging but which could be applied to seeing the world in a positive or negative light, as based upon assurance or as based upon fear. If the latter perspective is prevalent, it suggests that national security may not ever be wholly obtainable.

We must also note that in Maslow's original designation of his hierarchy, there was an emphasis on progression. As such, when applied to the individual, the basic physiological needs at the bottom of the pyramid were to be attained first before other higher needs could be realized. In contrast, in our analysis we related how these needs collectively form a set of requirements that an aspiring great power such as India is seeking to meet *simultaneously*. As such, elites are pursuing esteem and self-actualization needs at the same time as physiological and safety needs. Tellingly in this regard, and given the government's current shortcomings concerning these latter elements, it may be in India's national interest to fulfil Maslow's original intentions of first fully meeting basic needs, as only then will New Delhi be able to genuinely achieve its great power aspirations.

How Is India Doing?

As with all elements of national security, evaluating how well a country is doing in terms of meeting its core interests (and combating accompanying fears) is a relative process. On the most basic count, governing elites in India are far from meeting biological needs, with large portions of the population currently without sustained access to electricity, running water, and sanitation. That stated, New Delhi does guarantee some level of food security as well as rudimentary access to work so as to better achieve these safety needs along with family, health, and property needs. Large national and local security forces are present to counter myriad founts of instability and, along with her armed forces, seek to provide a safer and securer environment for India's citizens.

At the root of these issues is the size of India's population, which has always magnified such resource-based needs on a scale that only leaders in Beijing are familiar with. Decades of rapid economic growth are producing results though, and India is, without doubt, trying to develop and modernize many facets of its infrastructure. An outward-looking and outward-embracing economic policy is bolstering these aims and, if growth can be maintained, one will see the gradual amelioration in each of these areas. The modernization

128

process is also helping New Delhi in terms of fulfilling wider esteem and self-actualization needs, as more countries are recognizing India's dominant position in South Asia and her emergent/emerged position as a great power. As with the other levels, these needs are not yet fully resolved, especially regarding her potential.

Scale again plays a vital role by intensifying the threat posed by anything from insurgency to pollution, and is thus amplifying threats and incumbent fears to a level that would challenge any country. Among other issues, that over a tenth of her territory is contested, that an average of 2,000 people have died each year from terrorist and insurgent deaths since 1994, and that at least a million people are dying per year due to pollution, indicate the extreme size of her problems.

Such observations point to a few areas of contention. First, India is a country transitioning to become a developed and modern entity, and as such we ought to temper our criticism of her current record and standing. Secondly though, and conversely, we must ask if the huge range of national security tools that India possesses—institutionally, legally, militarily, economically, and diplomatically—are sufficient to meet the overload of national security threats that she faces.

Certainly, India has been censured on a number of occasions for not having the resources to adequately meet her national security needs. These include an under-prepared and slow response to the mass 2008 Mumbai attacks (despite receiving prior warning); having too insufficient a number of trained diplomats in the MEA; as well as modernizing her military forces without the necessary strategic overview, whereby even though it is spending vast sums on modernizing its forces and buying new weapons systems, there has been limited progress in general capabilities. Criticism of the conduct of her armed forces, widespread human rights abuses, and societal inequalities only add to the weight of denunciation that is periodically fixed towards India's elites.

At its most extreme—and when conveyed through the prism of thinking about national security interests with regard to the fears that challenge them—inadequate delivery in these areas can be seen to rest with those who are governing (and have governed) India. Certainly such an argument is pertinent domestically, concerning providing basic needs to India's population. By extension, incompetent leaders can thus be perceived as a national security threat in that they are/ were unable to protect national interests by effectively resolving the threats posed to them. Open political abuses such as corruption, nepotism, and patronage are the most egregious cases of such conduct. It is the virtue of (Indian) democracy that it is a mechanism for the population to remove such leaders.

Paradox and Parallax

Paradox: A statement containing two opposite ideas that make it seem impossible or unlikely, although it is probably true.

Parallax: The effect whereby the position or direction of an object appears to differ when viewed from different positions.

While we can be both understanding and critical of New Delhi's predicaments concerning the array of threats that she faces vis-à-vis her national security outlook, this treatise on Indian national security has also indicated an inherent quandary within such dynamics. This dilemma rests within the interactional aspect of our analytical stance, whereby security is a relational and relative exchange that occurs between actors. This dilemma rests within the interaction aspect of our analytical stance, whereby security is a relational and relative exchange that occurs between actors. So essential is this behaviour that if there were no such interaction there would be nothing for countries to be threatened by and thus nothing to fear. This contention brings us to two indispensable features of national security: paradox and parallax.

First, national security is a relational act that frequently, and necessarily, brings countries (and other actors) into conflict with each other. As such, what may be a national security prerequisite for generations of Indian leaders, say concerning the status of Jammu and Kashmir as being entirely part of the Indian land-mass, is diametrically opposed to it also concurrently being a precondition within, for instance, *Pakistani* national security. Applicable to almost any dispute or contestation, this innate tension produces the feature of *paradox* within national security analysis whereby there are competing but intractable claims for the same (material- or identity-based) end.

Secondly, this observation also highlights that national security—in terms of negatively pertaining to mutually incompatible interests and ambitions—is inherently concerned with difference. In this way it is very difficult for actors (of any kind, at the inter-national, national, or subnational level) to perceive the same issue, problem, fear, assurance, and desire in exactly the same way, especially if it relates to a specific paradoxical interaction between them. It is from this basis that our analysis of national security indicates a second feature—that of *parallax*—through which basic differences between those interacting fundamentally produces existential fear, threat, and danger.

When applied to the vicissitudes of contemporary domestic and international politics, and its constant evolution and adaptation as actors continually interact with each other, the features of paradox and parallax importantly show us that national security is never entirely in the singular control of its major actors. Thus, for India, if other neighbouring countries wish to contest their mutual borders, such issues will endure as a source of insecurity. Equally, if an insurgent group is unwilling to give up its alternative political or territorial image of India, they will also persist as a threat to New Delhi. In these ways, it is the aim of national and international diplomacy to produce outcomes that different parties are able to agree on and which meet their respective self-images.

Such a task is far from straightforward, especially as it is the interaction between actors itself that frequently leads to an emboldening—and potentially worsening—of relations, and which is majorly reliant upon the perceptions governing them. For instance, New Delhi may feel that it is necessary to modernize her military forces so as to protect India's trade and energy routes, and augment her international image as a developed great power. Such virtues are benign in isolation but may be seen as threatening by others (say Beijing), who then feel that they must also modernize their armed forces. Such interaction, even though rational and ostensibly peaceful in origin, is then the basis for an arms race and an insecurity spiral among two self-interested actors.

National (In)Security

Given these tensions, national security in its purest sense is a highly idealized sentiment. As domestic politics and international affairs rest upon interaction between actors in situations that are often paradoxical and zero-sum, the simultaneous attainment of complete security by all actors is impossible. At best, countries must balance achieving their national interests with some form of concession, which creates a more stable environment rather than exacerbating tensions. India's multi-pronged international diplomacy, especially her membership of different multilateral institutions that demand some loss of sovereignty, highlights the usefulness of such an attitude.

In this way, there is a limit to what New Delhi can achieve, both literally in terms of the threats she faces and fundamentally in terms of the general paradigm of national security. What is also clear is that the focus of national security—for policymakers and analysts alike—principally lies on its negative aspects. As such, as much as we can examine national security interests—those things that a country or actor would preferably like to accomplish—our discussion weighs more heavily on the threats towards these interests and the often deep-seated fears that they symbolize.

When taken together with paradox and parallax, such is the scale of these adverse features—especially when magnified by memory and imagination (of what might happen)—that there exists an *infinity of fear* between actors that no number of tools can fully compensate for. Within such an atmosphere, and given that it affects all actors at some direct or indirect level, rather than thinking of national security, we are in actual fact considering national insecurity. Therefore, and even if New Delhi can resolve most of the threats she currently faces, because of its essentially utopian nature, any study of her national security really remains that of Indian national insecurity.

Bibliography

Carbon Dioxide Information Analysis Center. 2015. 'Ranking of the World's Countries by 2011 Total CO2 Emissions'. Available at http://cdiac.ornl.gov/trends/emis/top2011.tot. Accessed on 10 May 2017.

Census of India. 2011. 'Distribution of Population by Religions', *Drop-in-Article on Census*, No. 4. New Delhi: Census of India, Ministry of Home Affairs. Available at http://censusindia.gov.in/Ad_Campaign/drop_in_articles/04-Distribution_by_Religion.pdf. Accessed on 10 May 2017.

Central Intelligence Agency. 2017. 'GDP (Purchasing Power Parity)', *CIA World Factbook*. Available at https://www.cia.gov/library/publications/the-world. Accessed on 10 May 2017.factbook/rankorder/2001rank.html.

————. 2017. 'India', *CIA World Factbook*. Available at https://www.cia.gov/library/publications/the-world-factbook/geos/in.html. Accessed on 10 May 2017.

Chibba, Michael. 2011. 'The Next Paradigm Shift in India and China?', *Asia-Pacific Economic Literature*, 25 (1): 152.

Conroy, Gerald P., Anil Kalhan, Mamta Kaushal, Jed S. Rakoff, and Sam Scott Miller. 2006. 'Colonial Continuities: Human Rights, Terrorism and Security Laws in India', *Columbia Journal of Asian Law*, 20 (1): 93–234.

Galtung, Johan. 1969. 'Violence, Peace, and Peace Research', *Journal of Peace Research*, 6 (3): 167–91.

Katzenstein, Peter J. 1996. *Cultural Norms and National Security: Police and Military in Post-War Japan*. Ithaca: Cornell University Press.

Khilnani, Sunil. 1997. *The Idea of India*. London: Hamish Hamilton.

Ladwig, Walter C. 2015. 'Indian Military Modernization and Conventional Deterrence in South Asia', *Journal of Strategic Studies*, 38 (5): 1–44.

Madisson, Angus. 2003. *The World Economy: Historical Statistics*. Paris: OECD Publishing.

Maslow, A.H. 1954. *Motivation and Personality*. New York: Harper and Row.

Ministry of Home Affairs (India). 1967. 'Unlawful Activities (Prevention) Act of 1967'. Available at http://mha. nic.in/sites/upload_files/mha/files/pdf/Unlawful_ Activities_Prevention_Act1967.pdf. Accessed on 10 May 2017.

————. 1980. 'National Security Act of 1980'. Available at http://mha.nic.in/sites/upload_files/mha/files/ National_Security_Act1980_270916.PDF. Accessed on 10 May 2017.

Ministry of Law and Justice. 2017. 'The Indian Constitution', *Ministry of Law & Justice (India)*. Available at http:// lawmin.nic.in/olwing/coi/coi-english/coi-indexenglish. htm. Accessed on 10 May 2017.

Nehru, Jawaharlal. 1946. *The Discovery of India*. New York: John Day.

Noronha, Ligia and Anant Sudarshan (eds). 2011. 'Contextualizing India's Energy Security', in *India's Energy Security*, pp. 3–18. London: Routledge.

Nye, Joseph S. 2004. *Soft Power: The Means to Success in World Politics*. New York: Public Affairs.

Ogden, Chris. 2009. 'Post-Colonial, Pre-BJP: The Normative Parameters of India's Security Identity, 1947–1998', *Asian Journal of Political Science*, 17 (2): 215–37.

—————. 2014a. *Hindu Nationalism and the Evolution of Contemporary Indian Security: Portents of Power*. New Delhi: Oxford University Press.

—————. 2014b. *Indian Foreign Policy: Ambition & Transition*. Cambridge: Polity.

—————. 2017. *China & India: Asia's Emergent Great Powers*. Cambridge: Polity.

Oxford Dictionaries. 2017. 'Parallax'. Oxford: Oxford University Press. Available at https://en.oxforddictionaries.com/definition/parallax. Accessed on 10 May 2017.

Oxford Learners Dictionaries. 2017. 'Paradox'. Oxford: Oxford University Press. Available at http://www.oxfordlearnersdictionaries.com/definition/english/paradox?q=paradox. Accessed on 10 May 2017.

Planning Commission. 2006. *Integrated Energy Policy: Report of the Expert Committee*. New Delhi: Government of India, Planning Commission.

Safi, Michael. 2017. 'All North Indian Cities Fail to Meet Air Quality Standards, Report Finds', *The Guardian*, 13 January. Available at https://www.theguardian.com/

world/2017/jan/13/all-north-indian-cities-fail-meet-air-quality-standards-report-finds. Accessed on 10 May 2017.

Scott, David. 2008. 'The Great Power "Great Game" between India and China: The "Logic of Geography"', *Geopolitics*, 13 (1): 1–26.

South Asia Terrorism Portal. 2017a. 'Fatalities in Left-Wing Extremism: 2005–2016'. Available at http://www.satp. org/satporgtp/countries/india/maoist/data_sheets/ fatalitiesnaxal05-11.htm. Accessed on 10 May 2017.

————. 2017b. 'India: Terrorist, Insurgent and Extremist Groups'. Available at http://www.satp.org/satporgtp/ countries/india/terroristoutfits/index.htm. Accessed on 10 May 2017.

————. 2017c. 'Indian Fatalities 1994–2016'. Available at http://www.satp.org/satporgtp/countries/india/ database/indiafatalities.htm. Accessed on 10 May 2017.

Stockholm International Peace Research Institute. 2017. 'SIPRI Arms Transfers Database'. Available at http:// www.sipri.org/databases/armstransfers. Accessed on 10 May 2017.

————. 2017. 'SIPRI Military Expenditure Database', *Stockholm International Peace Research Institute*. Available at http://www.sipri.org/research/armaments/milex/ milex_database. Accessed on 10 May 2017.

The Hindu. 2014. 'India's Staggering Wealth Gap in Five Charts', 8 December. Available at http://www.thehindu. com/data/indias-staggering-wealth-gap-in-five-charts/ article6672115.ece. Accessed on 10 May 2017.

Transparency International. 2014. '2014 Corruption Perceptions Index'. Available at http://www.transparency. org/cpi2014. Accessed on 10 May 2017.

US Energy Information Administration. 2016. 'India: International Energy Data and Analysis', Washington, DC. Available at http://www.eia.gov/beta/international/ analysis.cfm?iso=IND. Accessed on 10 May 2017.

Wolfers, Arnold. 1952. 'National Security as an Ambiguous Symbol', *Political Science Quarterly*, 67 (4): 481–502.

World Bank. 2016a. 'Life Expectancy at Birth, Total (Years)'. Available at http://databank.worldbank.org/data. Accessed on 10 May 2017.

————. 2016b. 'Poverty Headcount Ratio at $1.90 a Day (2011 PPP) (% of Population)'. Available at http:// databank.worldbank.org/data. Accessed on 10 May 2017.

Zhao, Hong. 2012. *China and India: The Quest for Energy Resources in the Twenty-First Century*. London: Routledge.

Further Readings and Websites

Adeney, Katharine and Andrew Wyatt. 2010. *Contemporary India*. Basingstoke: Palgrave Macmillan.

Benner, Jeffrey. 1984. *Structure of Decision: The Indian Foreign Policy Bureaucracy*. New Delhi: South Asia Publishers.

Cohen, Stephen P. 2002. *India: Emergent Power*. Oxford: Oxford University Press.

————. 2010. *Arming Without Aiming: India's Military Modernization*. Washington: Brookings.

Dixit, J.N. 2004. *Makers of India's Foreign Policy: Raja Ram Mohun Roy to Yashwant Sinha*. Delhi: HarperCollins.

Ganguly, Sumit. 1994. *The Origins of War in South Asia: Indo-Pakistani Conflicts since 1947*. Boulder: Westview Press.

—————. 2009. *India and Counterinsurgency: Lesson Learned*. London: Routledge.

Jaffrelot, Christophe (ed.). 2007. *Hindu Nationalism: A Reader*. Princeton: Princeton University Press.

Jain, B.M. (ed.). 2009. *Global Power: India's Foreign Policy, 1947–2006*. Lanham: Lexington Books.

Luce, Edward. 2006. *In Spite of the Gods: The Strange Rise of Modern India*. London: Little Brown.

Mahadevan, Prem. 2011. *The Politics of Counterterrorism in India: Strategic Intelligence and National Security in South Asia*. London: IB Tauris.

Malone, David. 2011. *Does the Elephant Dance?* New Delhi: Oxford University Press.

Mitra, Subrata K. 2011. *Politics in India: Structure, Process and Policy*. Oxford: Routledge.

Mohan, C. Raja. 2003. *Crossing the Rubicon: The Shaping of India's New Foreign Policy*. Delhi: Penguin.

Nayar, Baldev Raj and T.V. Paul. 2004. *India in the World Order: Searching for Major Power Status*. New Delhi: Cambridge University Press.

Panagariya, Arvind. 2011. *India: The Emerging Giant*. Oxford: Oxford University Press.

Pant, Harsh V. 2008. *Contemporary Debates in Indian Foreign and Security Policy: India Negotiates Its Rise in the International System*. London: Palgrave-Macmillan.

Scott, David (ed.). 2011. *Handbook of India's International Relations*. London: Routledge.

Tharoor, Shashi. 2012. *Pax Indica: India and the World in the 21st Century*. New Delhi: Allen Lane.

Websites

Delhi Policy Group: http://www.delhipolicygroup.com/

Institute for Defence Studies and Analyses: http://www.idsa.in/

Institute of Peace and Conflict Studies: http://www.ipcs.org/

Ministry of External Affairs: http://meaindia.nic.in/

Ministry of Commerce: http://commerce.nic.in/

Ministry of Defence: http://mod.nic.in/

Ministry of Home Affairs: http://mha.nic.in/

Observer Research Foundation: http://www.observerindia.com/

Prime Minister's Office: http://pmindia.nic.in/

South Asia Terrorism Portal: http://www.satp.org/

United Service Institution of India: http://www.usiof-org/

Index

About the Author

CHRIS OGDEN is a senior lecturer in Asian Security at the School of International Relations, University of St Andrews, Scotland, UK. He has previously taught at the universities of Edinburgh, Glasgow, and Durham, and is recognized as a fellow of the UK's Higher Education Academy, and is a senior research associate with the Foreign Policy Centre in London. His research interests include the relationship between national identity, international security, and domestic politics in South Asia (primarily India) and East Asia (primarily China). He is also engaged with the analytical uses of social psychology in International Relations. His publications include *China and India: Asia's Emergent Great Powers* (2017), *Indian Foreign Policy* (2014), and *Hindu Nationalism and the Evolution of Contemporary Indian Security: Portents of Power* (2014).